WYCKOFF 2.0: STRUCTURES, VOLUME PROFILE AND ORDER FLOW

COMBINING THE LOGIC OF THE WYCKOFF
METHODOLOGY AND THE OBJECTIVITY OF THE
VOLUME PROFILE

2nd edition

RUBÉN VILLAHERMOSA CHAVES

CONTENTS

INTRODUCTION

This third publication provides a continuation of the content from the first book titled "Trading and Investing for Beginners," which presents all the basic concepts that a beginner needs to be aware of; and from the second "The Wyckoff Methodology in Depth" which describes the Wyckoff Method in more detail as a tool for trading in financial markets.

In this book we will go one step further and deal with more complex concepts, incorporating new tools that use volume data, such as Volume Profile and the Order Flow, which will be very useful to us.

I strongly recommend that you assimilate all the concepts that are dealt with in my previous books before studying this one. Otherwise it could lead to some confusion or lack of understanding.

Who should read this book?

The content is complex and advanced, which is why this book has been written for experienced and demanding traders, who want to take a qualitative step in their trading, through the study of advanced tools for volume analysis, such as Volume Profile and Order Flow.

The universal nature of this method makes it accessible to all types of traders; short, medium and long term. However, it is day traders who will probably benefit the most, since many of the tools that we will study are aimed at the exploitation of short term inefficiencies.

What is Wyckoff 2.0 and why do you need this knowledge?

If you have come this far, you have almost certainly experienced the frustration of trading with dubious tools, such as indicators, traditional chartism or other methodologies, which claim to have almost magical properties. We have all been through this. It's normal; the industry is designed to take us down this path. Only a few manage to get off the beaten track, and after studying the Wyckoff Method you have taken your first steps toward doing so.

Wyckoff 2.0 is the natural evolution of the Wyckoff Method. It involves a combination of two of the most powerful concepts in Technical Analysis: the best price analysis together with the best volume analysis.

In this book you will gain an in-depth understanding of how financial markets trade, the B side that very few know about, but which is tremendously important in determining each and every single price movement.

Being aware of the existence of everything that will give you a more objective and comprehensive perspective of what is really happening in the market and that will provide you with a more critical point of view. If this really piques your interest, it will make you think about the usefulness of the tools used and very possibly allow you to reach clear conclusions about what should be incorporated into your trading approach.

Why this book and not any another?

Simply put: there is no other book like this one. You won't find this content even in expensive trading courses. You will learn to use tools created by and for professional traders.

For the price of this book, you have in your hands a training course that will help you to professionalize your approach to trading, by enabling you to forecast sound and accurate scenarios, giving your trades a better chance of success.

What will you learn?

Thanks to the study of advanced chart interpretation techniques, this book will allow you to discover a new dimension of technical analysis.

The complex tools that are taught here are not well known within the trading community, but their mastery will undoubtedly allow you to raise your trading several levels; providing you with improved results.

It is important to stress that these tools are still based on a real underlying logic, but at a much deeper level of understanding. What we're trying to do here is evaluate the interaction between supply and demand, between buyers and sellers, from a more complex, but also more objective, perspective.

We will follow this program:

• The **first** part of the book will cover advanced knowledge about how financial markets trade: the current trading ecosystem. The electronification of markets has changed the way participants interact, and has paved the way for other types of traders to enter the market in a multitude of different ways and with different intentions. This initial part of the book will describe the contextual framework in which today's markets move, enabling us to broaden our perspective about where we are and the difficulty that each of these elements incorporates into our daily trading.

• The **second** part will take an in-depth look at the importance of volume in today's markets. It will show how auction theory provides a universal framework that governs price movements, supported by an explanation of the Law of Supply and Demand as you have never studied it before. It will explain how order matching occurs down to the last detail, in order to understand the nature of advanced tools such as Order Flow.

• The **third** part takes a comprehensive look at the Volume Profile tool. It describes the fundamentals, theory, composition, types and forms of profiles; and presents some of the most important uses we can make of this tool. Without a doubt, this is one of the key sections of the book.

• The **fourth** part covers everything related to the Order Flow tool. Order matching presents a series of issues that will be explained as you go through the book so that, having reached this section, you will be able to apply this tool as objectively as possible. You will learn what the interpretation of Order Flow is based on and how to identify Order Flow patterns for day trading.

• The **fifth** part explains what Wyckoff 2.0 is and how best to apply it. You will discover how the synergy between the analysis of structures and the volume profile can provide you with high probability trading opportunities. The last section covers some advanced position management concepts, applied by experienced traders.

As I have done in my previous books, I once again want to emphasize the importance of keeping expectations low and proceeding with common sense. Neither this book, nor any other, nor any course, mentoring session or specialization, will guarantee that you become a successful trader or investor. This is a path that requires knowledge and experience. The first part – knowledge– continues here and now, with the advanced content you will find in this book. Studying its content will take you a step closer to achieving your objectives. But even once you have acquired all this knowledge, it won't be enough. You will still need experience. And for this there is no possible shortcut. You can only acquire experience with hours of screen time and hard work. I wish you good luck on your journey.

PART 1. TODAY'S TRADING ECOSYSTEM

The markets have undergone a paradigm shift and, thanks to technological advances, in just a few years we have seen how trading has gone from being carried out entirely by people on the floor to fully electronic operations. This has contributed to the emergence of new players, new ways of trading and even new markets in the world of investment..

Unquestionably, all of this has led to the democratization of investment, allowing access to retail traders, who would not have participated just a few years ago. In this regard, it is no coincidence that most retail traders lose. The entire industry is set up to ensure this is the case, so that their participation simply serves as yet another (very small) source of liquidity for the market.

It is important to keep your feet on the ground. The world of trading and investing is too complex for a home-based retail trader with an internet connection and a computer to make any significant return on their capital. The odds are stacked against them, starting with the fact that the situation is dominated by large institutions which dedicate huge amounts of money both to the development of powerful tools and to the hiring of the most skilled people.

We will now take a very basic look at some of the lesser-known aspects of the current trading ecosystem They are of some relevance, since they could influence our trading approach.

Types of Participants in Financial Markets

Familiarizing ourselves with those who have the ability to influence price movements puts us in a better position to make trading and investment decisions. The financial markets are made up of a whole host of agents. Their trading methods will differ, based on their needs at any specific time.

One of the biggest mistakes we can make is to think that all market movements are orchestrated by a single entity; or to classify traders as either professionals or non-professionals. When these terms are used, along with "strong hands" and "weak hands" it is in order to understand who has greater control of the market, not as a battle between institutions and retail traders. As we know, the latter can do little or nothing when it comes to the most traded assets.

Keep in mind that everything also depends on the volume traded in each particular asset. As that volume increases, more intervention will come from the big players.

For example, one of the largest assets traded worldwide, the American S&P 500 index, is almost entirely controlled by large institutions, with at least 90% of volume traded by these sources. This is a battle they wage among themselves. No trade can be executed unless one institution is willing to take one side of the position and another institution is willing to take the opposite side. The market wouldn't be able to move a single tick if there wasn't an institution behind each movement.

By contrast, assets that trade at very low volumes can be influenced by traders with less capacity. That is why I wouldn't recommended trading assets with low liquidity, to avoid possible manipulations.

Our objective, then, is to analyze the behavior of the chart, to try to determine on which side most of the institutional money lies.

Let's categorize the different market participants according to their intent:

Hedging

This involves executing financial trades aimed at canceling or reducing risk. These trades consist of the acquisition or sell of a product that is correlated with the asset on which the hedge is to be established.

While it is true that the main objective of hedging is to limit risk, it can also be used to secure a latent profit or preserve the value of a fixed asset. These traders don't care in which direction the price moves, since this is not part of their core business. They do not trade with any directional intention, but with a more long-term vision.

Although there are different ways of hedging, the most traditional one focuses on the producer.

• An example of this would be an airline company that buys oil futures as a way of balancing its fuel costs.

• Another example would be a large international import and export company that buying foreign exchange to hedge against possible price changes.

Market makers would also be included in this category, since they might go to the market in order to ensure the neutral risk of all their positions as a whole, depending on their needs.

Speculation

Unlike hedgers, who basically trade to reduce their exposure to risk, speculative traders actively take on risk when they open their positions.

If, given the current market conditions, they believe that the price of the asset in question is cheap, they will buy. And vice versa if they consider it to be expensive.

The sole aim is to obtain a profit from the price movement. This category includes hedge funds, investment funds, trading firms and, in general, any institution that trades directionally in the market to seek profitability. They trade under all sorts of different time frames and also execute trades using high-frequency algorithms.

They are the most active players in the financial market. They basically focus on finding liquidity zones as, due to the large volumes they move, they need to find a counterparty to match their orders.

There is a very common misconception that all institutions are profitable. Many of these institutions are the preferred prey of agents in financial markets, because they move significant amounts of money and may have a weak trading model.

Although they are not purely speculative, some options traders could be included in this category as, if they have a large open position in the options market, it is very likely that they will also go to the futures market to try to defend them, if necessary.

Arbitrage

This consists of taking advantage of the imperfections of the financial market. These traders see an inefficiency in prices and execute trades with the aim of correcting this and adjusting prices.

There are different forms of arbitrage: trading a single product, trading different correlated products, trading between different markets and even trading between contracts with the same and different expiration dates.

An example would be trading a decorrelation between two markets for the same asset, such as the spot market and the futures market. For example, the euro against the dollar (EURUSD) currency pair and the derivative in the futures market (6E). An arbitrage strategy will take advantage of the minuscule price difference that may exist between these two markets to obtain a profit.

Aside from this we also have the **Central Banks**. They have the greatest capacity since they determine the monetary policies of countries mainly through the establishment of interest rates.

Of the types we have looked at, the only one that would enter the market with the directional objective of adding pressure to one side or the other would be the speculative trader. The other forms of transaction would have a different intention but would also ultimately be represented on the price. The fact that not all trades are speculative is a very important factor to take into account. Many make the mistake of thinking that every trade has a directional interest behind it, and in most cases this is not true. There are many types of participants that interact in the market and the needs of each one are different.

In addition to the intention behind the trade, it is worth highlighting the different time frames used by one or other trader. While some take into account the short term, others apply medium or long-term strategies. The key point is that each and every one of the movements in the market is being supported by a large institution and that at any moment another may enter that has a longer-term perspective with a greater capacity to influence the price.

ELECTRONIC MARKETS

Since 2007 the exchanges have gone from being controlled by humans to fully automated, electronic environments. Really it is only computers which now handle the processing for matching orders.

Source: SIFMA Insights. Electronic Trading Market Structure Primer

With the emergence of new technologies, IT advances and regulatory changes to the financial world, speed when transmitting and receiving data has become increasingly important. So much so that, today, electronic trading accounts for most of the traded volume.

The most traded products such as futures, stocks and CDS indices are the most electronified; at 90%, 80% and 80% respectively. By contrast, corporate bonds are at the lower end of the spectrum, since they represent more tailor-made products, with investment grade and high yield bonds at levels of 40% and 25% respectively.

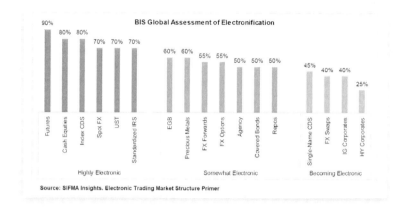

Source: SIFMA Insights. Electronic Trading Market Structure Primer

All these advances have made it possible to improve the efficiency of the market by adding liquidity, reducing costs, increasing the speed of execution, improving risk management and allowing access to specific markets.

Exhibit 2: Market Share of Algorithmic Trading by Asset Class

As of 2017.
Source: Goldman Sachs, AiteGroup

Algorithmic Trading

This is a process of executing orders based on well-defined and programmed rules, carried out automatically by a computer, with no human intervention.

It uses complex statistical and econometric models, on advanced platforms, to make decisions electronically and independently.

It mainly uses price, time and volume as variables and was developed to take advantage of the better speed and data processing offered by computers in comparison to human traders.

These strategies interpret market signals and automatically implement trading strategies based on these factors, with trades of different duration.

The increase in market share in the recent years of algorithmic trading across all types of assets is simply spectacular. Forecasts for the coming years are along the same lines.

One of the reasons for this growth is the emergence of artificial intelligence in the financial sector.

High-Frequency Trading

High-Frequency Trading is a type of algorithmic trading applied at the microsecond level, which aims to take advantage of very small changes in asset prices.

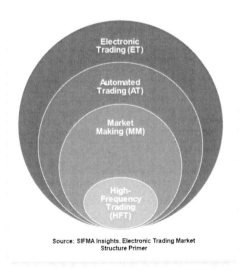

Source: SIFMA Insights. Electronic Trading Market Structure Primer

It is based on the use of mathematical algorithms, which are used to analyze the market and execute orders based on current conditions. They carry out thousands of trades in a short space of time, earning money systematically and with a high probability of success.

The main advantage is the speed of processing and execution, achieved thanks to the deployment of powerful computers. This means that amateur home-based traders simply do not have the means to access this type of trade. Therefore, it is a style reserved almost exclusively for institutional traders with large amounts of capital.

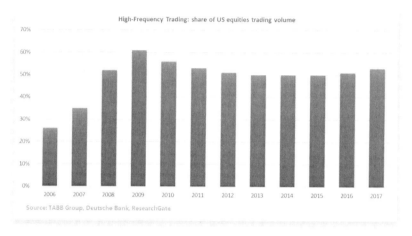

The share in the American stock market consistently represents over 50% of the total volume traded. In Europe it is slightly lower. It is worth noting how the 2009 crisis led to a decrease in the implementation of HFT, mainly due to increased competitiveness, high costs and low volatility.

Don't confuse High-Frequency Trading with the automatic systems that a retail trader might create (which do fall into the category of algorithmic trading). Generally these types of tools (known as EAs, robots or bots) are not usually very effective; unlike High-Frequency Trading tools, which cost millions of dollars and have been developed by large financial firms for daily trading with large amounts of money.

How do high-frequency algorithms affect us?

The fact that in today's markets most of the volume traded comes from high-frequency algorithms does not greatly influence the structure-based analysis that we can carry out. This is mainly because we are not competing to exploit the same anomalies.

While our analyses seek to take advantage of a deterministic aseptic of the market, where we try to elucidate who has more control (buyers or sellers), high-frequency algorithms are more geared towards the random aspect of the market, mainly due to their categorization: arbitrage, directional strategies (momentum and event-based) and market making (liquidity ratio).

Although it is true that some algorithms can execute directional strategies (with the aim of benefiting from price movements), these only cover the very short term. Although they could distort our analyses, the advantage of the Wyckoff Method is that it provides a structural framework, allowing us to minimize some of the noise found in the shorter time frames and to gain a more objective feel for current market conditions, by taking into account a larger context than these algorithms encompass.

OVER THE COUNTER (OTC) MARKETS

This is a type of electronic market where financial assets are traded between two parties without the control and supervision of a regulator, unlike in stock exchanges and futures markets.

The main difference between centralized markets (On-Exchange) and non-centralized markets (Off-Exchange) is that in centralized markets there is a single order book which is responsible for connecting all the participants of that market; while in non-centralized markets there are multiple order books (as many as there are market makers) where the lack of transparency regarding the depth of the market is made evident by the BID and the ASK price.

In recent years, the American market has undergone a process of fragmentation, in which more and more decentralized markets have been created. Currently, US stock liquidity is distributed between 88 different sources, with almost 40% of trades taking place in non-centralized markets.

Total Market Equity Share
Total volume based on October-November 2018

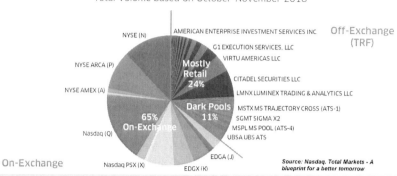

Non-centralized markets contain different types of broker, depending on the way they handle their clients' orders. On the one hand, there are those who have a dealing desk that act as the client's counterparty (known as Market Makers); and on the other those that do not have a dealing desk (Non Dealing Desk) that act as intermediaries between the client and the rest of the market.

This second type, non-dealing desk brokers, are the ones I recommend working with. The reason is that the Market Makers are in charge of offering the final price of the asset, making the process less transparent.

Since they can be the counterparty to their clients' trades, this opens up the possibility of a conflict of interest, because if the client wins, the broker loses and vice versa. And obviously the broker will do everything possible to ensure the profitability of their business.

When you combine the fact that the owner of the market is in charge of offering the final price and that they can be the counterparty at the same time, one of the main dangers for the retail trader is that they may suffer as a result of price movements being manipulated.

It is also important to know that, due to the very nature of this type of non-centralized market, there may be different prices for the same asset. In other words, if we want to trade the EUR/USD currency pair, each market maker will offer us a different price and volume.

How do OTC markets affect us?

The problem with these types of market is that our analyses will be based on data that might be a valid and significant representation of the market, but could just as easily not be representative of all price and volume data.

To guarantee the reliability of our data, we need to analyze the asset in question in a centralized market. Continuing with the example of the EUR/USD, we would need to analyze the futures market (centralized market) which corresponds to the ticker $6E.

Therefore, I recommend that if you do not have the economic capacity (sufficient capital) to trade in said futures market, you analyze the asset in this futures market and execute the trade through another more affordable financial derivative such as the CFD (Contract For Difference) with a good broker (not a market maker). An intermediate option would be to trade the small version of the future, the micro future, which, in the case of EURUSD, corresponds to the ticker $M6E.

If you open a chart for the future (6E) and the CFD (EURUSD) you will see that the price movements are practically the same, even though they are different markets. This is possible thanks to an arbitrage process carried out by high-frequency algorithms, which occurs systematically between both markets.

DARK POOLS

A Dark Pool is a private market (Off-Exchange) that puts institutional investors in contact with each other and facilitates the exchange of financial assets. What is particular about this sort of market is that the transactions are not reported immediately, and the amount traded (volume) is not disclosed for 24 hours.

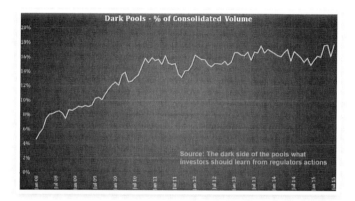

In the US, non-centralized markets represent approximately 35% of equity trading, with about 16 to 18% traded in Dark Pools. And according to a study by Bloomberg transactions in Dark Pools already represent over 30% of the total volume traded as a whole.

The market share of Dark Pools in European equity trading has expanded rapidly in recent years, growing from 1% in 2009 to 8% in 2016.

When a large institution wants to buy or sell a huge amount of an asset, it goes to this type of market. This is mainly because it knows that if it accesses the public market it will be difficult to find a counterparty and it will possibly obtain a worse price, while exposing itself to predatory techniques, executed by high frequency algorithms, such as Front Running. In this type of market traders avoid these negative effects and at the same time obtain better commissions since they save on the fees required by the public markets.

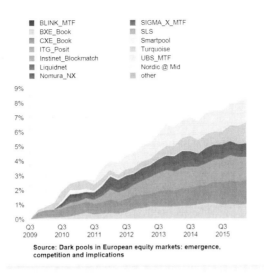

Source: Dark pools in European equity markets: emergence, competition and implications

Contrary to what many people may think, Dark Pools are highly regulated, since their owners are registered with the SEC (Securities and Exchange Commission) and FINRA (The Financial Industry Regulatory Authority) and therefore are subject to audits and regular examinations, similar to those of a public market.

In addition to private financial institutions, there are public exchanges that have their own Dark Pools, such as the New York Stock Exchange (NYSE), the most traded and liquid stock exchange in the world.

The CME (Chicago Mercantile Exchange), which is the market with the largest number of futures and options contracts in the world, also has its own Dark Pool and offers this opaque trading service through what they call "Block Trades". Its own website offers information on this matter, including the following:

"Block trades are privately negotiated futures, options or combination transactions that are permitted to be executed apart from the central limit order book. Only "Eligible Contract Participants" or ECPs are permitted to transact blocks. The qualifications are formally defined in the Commodity Exchange Act

Rule 526 ("Block Trades") governs block trading in CME, CBOT, NYMEX and COMEX products. Block trades are permitted in specified products and are subject to minimum transaction size requirements. These vary according to the product, the type of transaction and the time of execution. Block trades must be transacted at prices that are "fair and reasonable" in light of the size of the transactions, prevailing market prices in the futures and other related markets, and other relevant circumstances".

How do Dark Pools affect us?

The activity carried out in Dark Pools has important microstructural implications as it plays an important role in determining intraday returns and the uncertainty that may be related to them.

So we might be analyzing an asset in which very significant transactions have been carried out in a hidden manner and obviously we cannot even assess the intentions of the buyer.

Since they are not determined by the supply and demand of the public market, these transactions do not have an immediate impact on price formation. However, there are studies that claim that public market traders react to the report of orders executed in the Dark Pool once it is released, which can significantly alter the analysis of the interaction up to that moment.

RANDOMNESS VS DETERMINISM

This is another of the major debates that generates huge controversy among the trading community. The vast majority of those who position themselves in favor of the randomness of the market do so with the aim of discrediting technical analysis as a useful tool. On the other hand, we have those who look at each and every price movement and believe there is intent behind them all; a big mistake. Not everything is black or white.

Randomness is based on the premise of market efficiency. Determinism (non-randomness) is based on its inefficiency.

The random market approach implies that the current price already reflects all the information of the events that occurred in the past and even of the events that the market expects to take place in the future. That is, all the information about the asset is entirely discounted and therefore it is not possible to predict the future price action. The logic is that, when participants try to take advantage of new information, they mutually neutralize said advantage. This leads to the conclusion that there is no advantage to trying to interpret the market per se, unless the trader has access to insider information.

The deterministic market approach suggests that price movements are influenced by external factors, so by knowing what these factors are, the future price action can be predicted. Therefore profits can be obtained by correctly interpreting the market.

When we talk about randomness, we refer to the fact that there is no logical intent behind the movement of the market; it is simply a price fluctuation. Randomness is born of the innumerable variables that exist in the market. No one can possibly know how the rest of the market participants are going to act. If someone knew, they would implement a deterministic system to predict the right outcome every single time.

On the one hand, if the Efficient Market Hypothesis (EMH) and the randomness of the market were valid, no one would be able to obtain profits on a recurring basis. And history has shown that this is not the case. We all know big players in the financial markets who have managed to win with different approaches (technical, fundamental and quantitative). Moreover, the efficient markets hypothesis is heavily criticized because it assumes agents act rationally in all their decision making.

On the other hand, financial markets cannot be modeled as a totally deterministic process in which there is no randomness. This would result in strategies with 100% probability of success and this (as far as we know) is not the case.

The Adaptive Market Hypothesis

We are, therefore, led to the conclusion that financial markets are made up of a percentage of randomness and a percentage of determinism, though we cannot attribute a proportion to each.

This theory is supported by the Adaptive Market Hypothesis (AMH) which shows the efficiency of financial markets, not as a characteristic that either exists or doesn't exist, but as a quality that varies according to market conditions (the environment, context), which are determined by the interactions between agents.

This hypothesis was presented by the American financial economist Andrew W. Lo in his book Adaptive Markets published in 2017 and is mainly based on the following points:

• **The efficiency of the market depends on its condition**. This changing characteristic is the result of the interactions of the participants, which in turn depend on market conditions.

• **The agent is not fully rational and is subject to cognitive biases**. Participants form expectations based on different factors. For this reason a purely rational model cannot be applied. Moreover, different expectations may be created based on the same information, not to mention the fact that each agent is risk averse to a different extent.

Although the author refers to agents as individual people, this is equally applicable to the current trading ecosystem in which, as we have already mentioned, practically all actions are carried out electronically, by algorithms. This doesn't alter the principle of the adaptive hypothesis. Regardless of who the market participant is and the way in which it interacts with the rest of the market, it will make its decisions based on the valuations, motives or needs that it has at a given moment. That given moment will be conditioned by different factors, factors that will change over time and therefore change the evaluations, motives or needs of the participants.

AMH doesn't focus on discrediting the Efficient Markets Hypothesis, it simply treats it as incomplete. It places more value on changing market conditions (due to the emergence of new information) and how participants can react to these. It focuses on the fact that rationality and irrationality (efficiency and inefficiency) can coexist in the market at the same time, depending on the conditions.

How does the Wyckoff methodology fit in?

Moving on to what really concerns us, interpreting the market under the principles of the Wyckoff Method is based on a deterministic market event: The law of Cause and Effect. Because for the market to develop an effect (trend) a cause (accumulation/distribution) must first have occurred. There are other deterministic events that can offer an advantage, such as seasonality.

An example of random behavior could be seen in High Frequency Algorithms. We have already discussed some of their uses and they are the perfect example of forces that have the ability to move the market without necessarily having any directional logic behind them.

Finally, it is worth noting that most studies defending the randomness of the market use traditional chartist patterns such as triangles, head and shoulders, flags, etc. or some price pattern with no underlying logic behind it, to confirm the lack of predictability of technical analysis in general. Our approach to trading the markets is far removed from all of this.

There are studies that have shown how, using a tool as simple as trend lines, you can observe non-random behavior in financial markets, and even exploit anomalies to obtain some return.

PRICE VS VOLUME

In our way of understanding how to analyze the market, we cannot initially conceive of doing so without knowing either the price or volume data. But as you delve deeper into the financial world's ecosystem, certain obstacles begin to emerge.

To put it succinctly, I believe that over time price data is certainly more relevant than volume data. And I will argue this based on two elements.

First, the intraday volume that we can analyze for any asset can be very misleading, depending on the moment of the session. For example, at the opening of the American session of the S&P500 at its local time (ETH), we will always see high volume, much higher than that seen prior to that opening during regular hours (RTH). And of course, all the previous analysis will be biased in some way.

As we can see in the ES chart (S&P500 futures), the greatest volatility and therefore price movement occurs during the American session, with a very clear lack of participation during regular hours. It wouldn't make much sense for our analysis to take into account all global price and volume action, because this could lead to confusion.

It is not that during regular hours we have identified a movement with a lack of interest (low volume); it is simply that the low volume is due to an absence of traders at that time. The same would happen during other moments of the session, such as at the pause at midday or just before starting the final stretch of the day, at which time there is also a significant increase in volume.

Once we understand this, there are two ways of resolving the situation:

• If we want to continue trading on intraday time frames we must necessarily analyze price and volume in comparative terms; looking at both the price and volume during local time and the same information during regular hours.

• Also, the best way to avoid confusion is to analyze the daily chart. Since this time frame covers both sessions (ETH and RTH), there is no need to distinguish between them for analysis. But of course, this would require a complete overhaul of your trading style.

The one thing that already incorporates all the information is the price. The price is the graphical representation of all the orders already executed. We could be analyzing an asset at any time and the price action would be faithfully reflected, without needing to know what moment of the session we're looking at or needing to carry out a comparative analysis. This is the advantage offered by the price.

Another factor that shows the importance of price over vertical volume is that the latter is ambiguous in its interpretation at times, and will always be subject to how the price reacts subsequently. As I explained in my analysis on Law of Effort and Result in my previous books, a certain behavior will indicate harmony or divergence depending on what the market does subsequently, and we will adapt our interpretation based on this. For example, if we see that the market moves accompanied by a lot of volume, we will say that it represents intent in that direction; that the market is moving because there is a great deal of interest in that movement. But if, on the contrary, we see that the market moves with the same price characteristics, but this time accompanied by a relatively low volume, we will say that this is because one of the sides (buyers or sellers) is not interested in participating, and that lack of interest favors a movement to the opposite side.

And both interpretations would be correct. The problem is that we could be misled into thinking that the movement with little volume behind it is a divergence when in fact it is because those driving it need very little commitment to move the price in that direction, due to the absence of traders on the opposite side.

Although we lose a large part of the available information without the volume, the continuous interaction between supply and demand leaves its mark on the price, and this develops certain repetitive patterns (not in form, but in substance).

Obviously trading without analyzing the volume data is not recommended for traders who use structures and VSA. Although it can sometimes result in ambiguous analyses, generally it enables us to identify the appearance of unbalancing events in the market. I simply want to emphasize the prevalence of price over volume for our way of understanding and trading the markets.

Furthermore, as we have seen previously, the appearance of Over The Counter (OTC) markets and Dark Pools add another layer of opacity when trying to properly interpret volume data.

THE ADOPTION/DIFFUSION MODEL

This model is a theory developed by sociologist Everett Rogers in 1962, in which he hypothesized how innovations spread from their introduction to their widespread adoption.

Dr Hank Pruden, a prominent Wyckoff trader, adapted this model to the functioning of financial markets in his book "The Three Skills of Top Trading". His idea was to combine the four elements of technical analysis (price, volume, time and sentiment) to represent a more complete and binding conclusion about the current position of a market and its likely future trend.

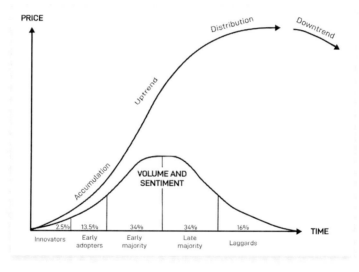

The base diagram is made up of two factors:

S-shaped curve

This represents the behavior of the price. The chart highlights the importance of the market cycle and its stages: accumulation, uptrend, distribution, and downtrend.

At this stage the reader will already be familiar with the basics of the development of a price cycle, so we will not delve into them further. If this is not the case, take a look at my previous books in which I provide a detailed explanation of the essence of price movement both contexts of the market: ranges and trends.

The market cycle is nothing more than a chart representation of the sequential participation of the different types of traders.

Gaussian bell curve

Represents the distribution of volume and sentiment. The chart identifies the number of market participants that join the trend in each period or category. Using this and an objective analysis of the data, we can determine in which phase of the Gaussian bell curve we are most likely to be in any particular market.

Categories depending on the moment of adoption of the trend:

• **Innovators**. This category comprises 2.5%. In the financial market, the innovators are the Insiders. Due to their delicate position, it is very difficult to detect their participation and correctly interpret the intention behind their actions.

• **Early adopters**. 13.5% of the total. These are the smartest traders of today. They are well-informed traders. They have basically performed objective valuations of the assets and are positioned in expectation of the price travelling a great distance. They are also those technical traders who have been able to correctly identify institutional intervention and position themselves alongside these major players.

• **Early majority**. This covers 34% of the population. These are well-informed traders who have been able to correctly and quickly identify the start of the cycle and position themselves in the early phases.

• **Late majority**. The other 34% of the distribution. Not very well informed traders who react slowly by going to the market at a very late phase of the movement.

• **Laggards**. The remaining 16%. These are the least informed traders and they are also guided by their emotions. They are attracted to the trend in its final phase and open positions at the end of the cycle.

The S-shaped curve and the normal distribution together make up what Pruden called "The Life Cycle Model of Crowd Behavior."

The key is to observe the impact this has on the market, and how the process of participation or adoption of a trend is represented on the chart as the different categories of traders enter or leave the market:

• **Innovators and Early Adapters = Accumulation/Distribution Process**. Specific field of study of the Wyckoff Method. It is in this construction of the cause that we try to determine whether these well-informed early participants are building a buying (accumulation) or selling (distribution) position.

• **Early Majority = Early phases of the rend movement**. They enter once the trend has started. The price won't run the same distance in their favor as with the previous category, but they are certainly entering at a very favorable point in the movement and if they are able to objectively analyze the health of the trend. They can make a big profit.

• **Late majority = End of the trend movement**. This is where the most volume can be observed, so this continues to attract a larger number of participants to the market. This creates a mutually reinforcing spiral: volume expansion and price displacement. As prices rise, more buyers are attracted; and as prices fall, more sellers are attracted. In other words, buying and selling waves tend to snowball. But there is little distance left for the price to travel.

• **Laggards = Reversal**. The last participants are drawn to the market by greed, for fear of missing out on the movement. They are generally those who doubted the validity of the trend, were skeptical and didn't want to enter at a previous point. They enter the wrong side of the market and subsequently take huge losses.

This model can be seen in every market cycle, in each accumulation and distribution process, whose cause has a subsequent respective upward and downward trend effect.

In essence, it represents the ideal behavior of what a healthy trend movement should look like, in terms of the evaluation of price action and volume: increasing volume in the early stages of the trend and decreasing volume in the later stages, denoting exhaustion.

Free gift #1: Video: Types of participants.

To complement the content in this section, I'm offering you a video where I explain the different types of market participants and which among them truly have the capacity to influence asset prices.

You can access from this link: https://tradingwyckoff.com/book-2/

or by scanning this QR code directly::

PART 2. THE IMPORTANCE OF VOLUME

A s we already seen, volume is a far more significant factor in today's markets than it was in previous decades. More and more money is being moved through every financial market and this has resulted in certain changes; from the way people trade to the emergence of new tools.

At the beginning of the 20th Century, the markets operated entirely manually and were guided mainly by the cognitive biases of their participants. Emotions such as fear and greed would rear their ugly heads and influence a large part of the decision-making carried out by market participants. This irrationality of the individual led to very beneficial situations for the well-informed trader at that time.

As everyone now knows, today's ecosystem is one in which the vast majority of volume is traded electronically, in which huge amounts of volume are moved daily and in which the concepts of counterparty, liquidity and order matching are of the utmost relevance if all these orders are to be fulfilled; in short, the importance of volume.

This section will offer a detailed study of auction theory and take a look at some tools that will allow us to more accurately analyze volume data.

AUCTION MARKET THEORY

The origins of auction theory can be found mainly in the studies on Market Profile carried out by J.P. Steidlmayer. Steidlmayer, together with other authors such as James Dalton and Donald L. Jones, later defined a series of concepts that constitute said theory.

It is based on the fact that the market, with the primary aim of **facilitating trading** among its participants and under the principles of the law of supply and demand, will always move in search of efficiency, also known as balance or fair value.

Efficiency indicates that buyers and sellers are comfortable trading and neither has clear control. That comfort arises from the fact that, based on current market conditions, the valuations of both are very similar. This balance is visually represented on a price chart through the continuous pivoting of the price (within price ranges). These sideways price movements represent said balance. It is the evidence of a context in which trading is being facilitated, the state which the market is always attempting to reach.

Then we have moments of **inefficiency** or Imbalance. These are represented through the trend movements. When new information reaches the market, it can cause the value of said asset, as perceived by both buyers and sellers, to change, generating a disagreement between them. One of the two will take control and move the price away from the previous balance zone, offering us a trading opportunity. What is evident in this context is that the market is not facilitating trading and therefore it is deemed to be in an inefficient condition.

The market will be constantly moving in search and confirmation of the value; in situations where buyers and sellers are in a position to exchange stocks. When this happens, it is because the valuations that these participants have regarding price are very similar. At that moment, trading activity will once again generate a new zone of balance. This cycle will be repeated over and over again without interruption.

The general idea is that the market will move from one **balance** zone to another, through trend movements, and that these will start when the market sentiment of both buyers and sellers regarding current value differs, causing the **imbalance**. The market will now start searching for the next area that generates consensus regarding value, among the majority of participants.

It is worth noting that the market spends most of its time in periods of balance. This is logical, since it is the nature of the market to promote trading among its participants. This is where those accumulation and distribution processes take place, which, as we all know, is the focus of the Wyckoff Method.

Variables

The auction process in financial markets is fundamentally based on value. To try to determine where said value is found, three additional elements need to be evaluated:

Price

In the auction mechanism, the price is used as an exploratory tool. The negotiation is facilitated through the movement of the price, which fluctuates up and down, exploring the different levels in order to see how the participants react to said probing.

These price movements herald opportunities. After this probing the participants will start to trade with each other, if they believe the price to be fair. Conversely, if this exploration of new price levels is not perceived as attractive for both participants, it will be rejected.

Time

When the market offers an opportunity (reaches an attractive level), it will use time to regulate the duration that the opportunity will be available.

The price will spend very little time in those areas that are advantageous for one of the two sides (buyers or sellers).

An efficiency or balance zone will be characterized by a greater consumption of time; while an area of inefficiency or Imbalance will last for a shorter period of time.

Volume

The volume represents the activity; the amount of an asset that has been exchanged. This quantity indicates the interest or disinterest there is at certain price levels.

There are zones that are more valuable than others, based on the volume. The basic rule of thumb is that the more activity observed in a given area, the higher the value placed on it by market participants.

Price + Time + Volume = Value

These three elements provide us with a rational perspective regarding where market participants consider the value of a particular asset to be based on current conditions.

The market explores new levels using the price. The consumption of time suggests that there is a certain acceptance in this new area and finally the generation of volume confirms that the participants have created a new zone of value where they trade comfortably.

As we know, conditions are always changing, so these elements need to be continuously re-assessed. Knowing where the value is key since it defines the condition of the market. We can then take different approaches to trading, based on this.

Perception of Value

The market is constantly pivoting between two phases: horizontal development (balance) and vertical development (Imbalance). Horizontal development suggests an agreement between participants, while vertical development is a market in search of value, in search of participants with whom to trade.

The fact that the price is moving comfortably in a trading range (horizontal development) represents acceptance in said zone; a context where price and value coincide according to the participants. When the market is in a trend situation (vertical development) price and value do not coincide. In this context the price will move first and the value may follow or not (as a sign of acceptance or rejection).

In an balance zone, the fairest price will be located in the middle and the two extremes, both above and below, will represent unfair levels or levels not accepted by the participants.

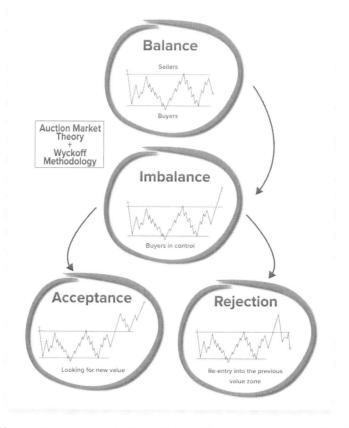

If the fairest value is in the middle of the range, a move to the higher end will be seen by buyers as expensive, while sellers will see it as cheap, and their actions will send the price back to the fairest area. Similarly, a visit to the lower end of the range will be seen as cheap for buyers and expensive for sellers, which will lead to a new reversal upwards.

This is what is commonly known as range trading, where traders look to buy at the lows and sell at the highs, hoping that the price will continue to reject these extremes. And normally the market will continue like this until its condition changes.

What is interesting is when Imbalance occurs and the price leaves the value area. What happens then? When the price leaves a trading zone, a change in the perception of value may take place.

The trader's task is now to assess whether these new price levels will be accepted or rejected. Price moves ahead of the other two variables in determining potential value areas, but it is time in the first instance and volume in the last, that will confirm whether a new area is accepted or rejected.

We interpret acceptance of a new area when the price manages to stay at that level (it consumes more time) and contracts between buyers and sellers begin to be exchanged (volume), with all this represented by a certain sideways movement of the price. By contrast, we would identify rejection when the price quickly reverts back to its old value area, denoting a lack of interest and evidenced by a sharp reversal.

All horizontal developments end when there is no longer agreement between the participants about the value; while all vertical developments end when the price reaches an area where there is agreement between them once again. This is the continuous cycle of the market. This idea in itself is very powerful and, with the right approach, you could build trading strategies around it.

As with one of the universal principles of technical analysis (the market discounts everything), we don't really need to analyze why this change in the perception of value by the participants takes place. We know that based on current conditions and the information available at that precise moment in time, all the participants value the price of the asset in a certain way. Something may then happen at a fundamental level that changes said perception, but the advantage of this approach is that we don't need to know and interpret what has happened for the participants to have changed their perception.

It is important to note that auction theory is universal and can be applied in the evaluation of any type of financial market, regardless of the time frame in question.

The Four Steps of Market Activity

This is a process with which Steidlmayer represented the different phases through which the market passes during the development of its movements.

The four phases are:

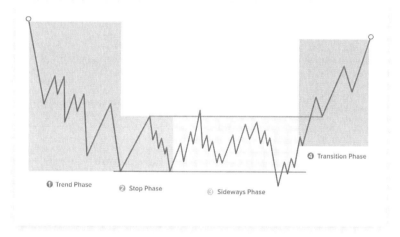

- **Trend phase**. Vertical development, Imbalance of price in favor of one direction.

- **Stop phase**. Traders in the opposite direction start to appear and the previous trend movement is stopped. Upper and lower range limits are set.

- **Sideways phase**. Horizontal development. Trading around the stop price and within the limits of the new balance range.

- **Transition phase**. The price leaves the range and generates a new Imbalance in search of value. Said movement may be a reversal or continuation of the previous trend movement.

Once the transition phase is over, the market is in a position to start a new cycle. This protocol will develop uninterruptedly and is observable in all time frames.

Visually, until step three, a P or b shaped profile will be observed. We will look in more detail later on at how the shape of this profile is generated and what trading approach should be adopted here.

For structure traders, this four-phase protocol will be familiar, since in essence it is exactly the development from Phase A to Phase E proposed by the Wyckoff methodology:

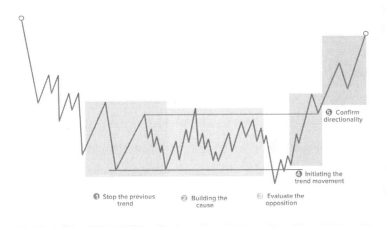

- **Stopping the previous trend**

- **Constructing the cause**

- **Assessing the opposition**

- **Starting the trend movement**

- **Confirming the direction**

Although Richard Wyckoff, as well as his later students and other traders who have contributed to the dissemination of his ideas, worked solely on the basis of analytical tools and technical analysis principles, we can see that they were already implicitly applying these auction theory concepts, even if they didn't use these exact same terms.

For this reason we consider using the only technical analysis approach that is based on a real underlying logic: auction theory and the law of supply and demand.

THE LAW OF SUPPLY AND DEMAND

This is the fundamental law on which auction theory is based and therefore governs all price changes. Richard Wyckoff's work initially claimed that said law suggested the following:

- If demand was greater than supply, the price of the product would rise.

- If the supply was greater than the demand, the price of the product would fall.

- If supply and demand were in balance, the price of the product would remain the same.

Common Errors of Interpretation

This idea is very general and needs to be qualified, since a series of conceptual errors have been generated around this law of supply and demand.

Error no. 1: Prices rise because there are more buyers than sellers or they fall because there are more sellers than buyers.

There are always the same number of buyers and sellers in the market because for someone to be able to buy there must be someone able to sell. No matter how much someone is interested in buying, if there is no seller willing to act as the counterparty, it is impossible for the transaction to take place.

The key lies in the attitude (aggressive or passive) that traders adopt when it comes to participating in the market.

Error no. 2: Prices rise because there is more demand than supply or they fall because there is more supply than demand.

The issue with this claim is dubbing everything that has to do with buying as demand and everything that has to do with selling as supply. In reality these are two different concepts and it is worth distinguishing between them when referring to one or the other.

Supply and Demand are the limit orders that both buyers and sellers place in the BID and ASK columns, which are left pending execution, otherwise known as liquidity.

BID/ASK, Spread and Liquidity

In financial markets there is no one single price. This may seem obvious, but it is something that a lot of people don't understand. When a participant goes to the market, they will be presented with two prices: the buy price and the sell price.

• **BID**. The BID column is the part of the order book where buyers go to place their order (buy limit orders) and where sellers go to match their sell orders. The highest price within the BID column is known as the Best BID and represents the best price at which the security can be sold.

• **ASK**. The ASK column is the part of the order book where sellers go to place their pending sell orders (offer) and where buyers go to find the counterparty for their buying. The lowest price within the ASK column is known as the Best ASK and represents the best price at which the asset can be bought.

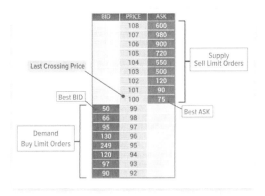

Therefore, it is the order execution mechanism that determines the price. The difference between the BID and the ASK is called the **Spread** and it is an indicator of the liquidity of said asset. The lower the Spread, the more liquid the asset.

Liquidity is an extremely important concept. It is the amount of volume an asset trades at. You should bear in mind that the more liquid the assets you trade the better, as it is less likely that a large trader will be able to individually impact the price. It is therefore a measure to avoid possible manipulation. If you are trading an asset that trades at very little volume, a large institution will most likely be able to move the price with relative ease. These environments should be avoided.

Types of Participants Based on Their Behavior

A key factor which helps clarify the errors of interpretation of the Law of Supply and Demand is the behavior of the traders, who can participate in the market in different ways:

• **Aggressively**. Liquidity takers who do so through "market" orders. They are anxious to enter immediately and attack the Best BID and the Best ASK prices where the limit orders are pending execution. These types of aggressive orders are the true driver of the market because they initiate the transactions.

• **Passively**. Liquidity providers who do so through "limit" orders. Sellers create supply by placing their pending orders in the ASK column; and buyers create demand by placing their orders in the BID column.

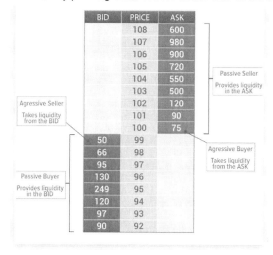

How Do Price Movements Occur?

We have now reached the point where should look at what has to happen for the price to move. The key is obvious; the aggressive participation of traders is necessary to produce a change in the price. Passive orders initially represent intent. If they end up being executed, they have the ability to stop a price movement but not the ability to generate one. This requires initiative.

Initiative

For the price to move higher, buyers have to acquire all the sell orders (supply) that are available at that price level and also continue to buy aggressively, to force the price to go up one level and there find new sellers to trade with.

Passive buy orders slow down the bearish movement, but they cannot drive the price up by themselves. The only orders that have the ability to move the price up are market buy orders or those that become market buy orders through the matching of orders (such as a Stop Loss on short positions).

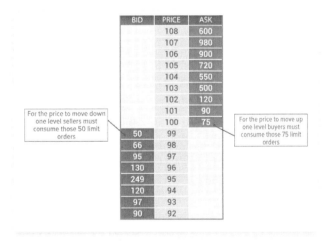

For the price to move lower, sellers have to acquire all the buy orders (demand) that are available at that price level and continue to put pressure downwards, forcing the price to search for buyers at lower levels.

Passive sell orders slow the bullish movement, but do not have the ability to bring the price down on their own. The only orders that have the ability to move the price down are market sell orders or those that become market sell orders through the matching of orders (Stop Loss on long positions).

Exhaustion

The price needs aggressiveness to move, but it is also worth noting that a lack of interest from the opposite side can help pave the way for this.

An absence of supply can help the price to rise in the same way that an absence of demand can cause it to fall.

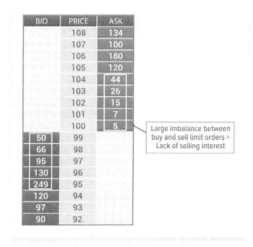

Large imbalance between buy and sell limit orders = Lack of selling interest

When the supply is withdrawn, this lack of interest will be represented as a smaller number of contracts placed in the ASK column and therefore the price may move more easily upwards with very little buyer power.

By contrast, if it is the demand that is withdrawn, this will translate into a reduction in the contracts that buyers have placed in the BID column and this will cause the price to fall with very little initiative from sellers.

How Do Market Reversals Occur?

Remember that the market, in order to facilitate trading, will go up looking for sellers and down looking for buyers; or put another way, it will always move towards the balance point in which supply and demand are equal.

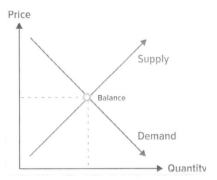

Moreover, by this logic, as the price rises, the interest of buyers decreases (they see the price as more and more expensive) and the interest of sellers increases (they see the price as cheaper and cheaper); and as the price falls, the interest of sellers decreases and that of buyers increases.

In an upward moving market, as long as the initiative of buyers is able to consume all the liquidity (supply) that is in the upper levels, the price will continue to rise. Meanwhile, in a bearish market, as long as the initiative of sellers is able to consume all the liquidity (demand) it finds at lower levels, the price will continue to fall.

A market reversal usually follows a three-step process:

1. **Exhaustion.**

2. **Absorption.**

3. **Initiative.**

The reversal of an upward movement involves a combination of a lack of interest (exhaustion) from buyers to continue buying, the first entry by large traders looking to sell in a passive way (absorption) and the aggressiveness (initiative) of sellers.

The opposite is true for the reversal of a downward movement: exhaustion of sellers, passive positioning through the selling absorption, and buying initiative with ASK aggression.

In essence, this three-step protocol is nothing more than an accumulation or distribution process regardless of the time scale in which it develops.

TYPES OF ORDERS

There are basically four different types of orders involved when participating in the market.

• **Market**. An aggressive order that is executed when the best buy and sell price is available (Best BID/ASK). An immediate order, guaranteeing the entry into the market but not the specific price of entry, due to the constant change in price and the application of the Spread.

• **Limit**. A passive order that is executed at a specific price. Entry or exit at that particular price is guaranteed but execution is not guaranteed. In other words, the price might never reach the desired level and therefore we wouldn't enter the market. It can be canceled at any time, as long it hasn't been executed.

• **Stop**. A passive order that is executed at a specific price. When this price is reached, it becomes a market order and is therefore executed at the best available price (Best BID/ASK).

• **Stop-Limit**. This combines the characteristics of Limit and Stop orders. Once a certain price level is reached (function of a Stop order), an order is generated at a specific level (function of a Limit order). Operationally it works in the same way as Limit orders.

Following on from the four types of orders we have just seen, the list below describes the full range of basic orders available according to intention and use:

• **Buy Market**. Aggressive order at the current price. Used for:

    • Entering the market to buy.

    • Closing a sell position (either at a profit or loss).

• **Buy Stop**. Pending order above the current price. Used for:

    • Entering the market to buy.

    • Closing a sell position (due to a Stop Loss)

• **Buy Limit**. Pending order below the current price. Used for:

    • Entering the market to buy.

    • Closing a sell position (due to a Take Profit)

• **Buy Stop Limit**. Pending order below the price after reaching a certain limit. Used for:

    • Entering the market to buy.

    • Closing a sell position (due to a Take Profit)

• **Sell Market**. Aggressive order at the current price. Used for:

    • Entering the market to sell.

    • Closing a buy position (either at a profit or loss).

• **Sell Stop**. Pending order below the current price. Used for:

    • Entering the market to sell.

- Closing a buy position (due to a Stop Loss)

- **Sell Limit**. Pending order above the current price. Used for:

    - Entering the market to sell.

    - Closing a buy position (due to a Take Profit)

- **Sell Stop Limit**. Pending order above the price after reaching a certain limit. Used for:

    - Entering the market to sell.

    - Closing a buy position (due to a Take Profit)

Advanced Characteristics

Depending on the broker, there are certain advanced instructions that can be applied to orders to enter and exit the market:

One-Cancels-Other (OCO). Introduction of two orders to the market, one of which is canceled when the other is executed.

Order-Sends-Order (OSO). Instruction to execute secondary orders when the initial one is executed.

Market-To-Limit (MTL). Execution of a market order that includes an instruction to place a limit order at the same price as the rest of the position in the event that it is not fully executed.

Market-If-Touched (MIT). Conditional order that becomes a market order when a specific level is reached. It is used to buy below the current price and to sell above the current price.

Limit-If-Touched (LIT). Conditional order that becomes a limit order when a specific level is reached. It is used to buy above the current price and to sell below the current price.

Good-Till-Cancelled (GTC). This order includes an execution period that is usually the duration of the session. If at that point the order has not been executed, it will be cancelled.

Good-Till-Date (GTD). The order remains active until a specific date.

Immediate-Or-Cancel (IOC). Instruction to execute the order immediately. If any portion of the order remains unfilled, that portion is cancelled.

Fill-Or-Kill (FOK). Does not allow partial execution. When the price reaches the desired level, the order is either executed with all the volume fulfilled or it is canceled.

All-Or-None (AON). Similar to FOK orders with the difference that if the price reaches the desired level and it is not executed because not all the volume can be covered, it continues to remain active until either it obtains all the counterparty or the trader cancels it.

At-The-Opening (ATO). Instruction to execute an order at the opening of the session. If this is not possible, it is canceled.

At-The-Close (ATC). Instruction to execute an order at the close of the session.

ADVANCED CHARTS

In recent years, new forms of representing the activity of the market have emerged. These new charts include tick charts, volume charts and range charts.

The main advantage of these charts is that they reduce the noise found in charts with specific time frames. A common feature of these three types of charts is that they ignore the time variable, which can be very useful, precisely for conditions such as those described above, in which the market covers different environments.

Tick Charts

A tick represents a transaction, a trade between two parties. The tick chart will be updated (the current candlestick will be closed and a new one will be opened) when a certain number of trades (ticks) have taken place.

The chart settings (the number of ticks) will vary between markets as volatility is different from market to market. As a result, you should carry out different tests until you find the ones most suitable for you.

In general, the volume will be very similar across all the generated candlesticks but there will be subtle differences that can provide us with interesting information, since this type of chart measures the activity in terms of transactions, but does not take into account the volume or amount traded in those transactions.

In other words, a chart set to 1000 ticks will generate a new candlestick when those 1000 ticks take place, but the amount traded in those thousand trades will differ. One or several contracts may be traded in any given transaction.

Volume Charts

The difference between the tick and volume charts has to do with the amount traded. While a tick chart measures the number of transactions without taking into account how many contracts, shares or units have been traded in each of them, a volume chart measures the number of contracts, shares or units traded before the generation of a new candlestick.

For example, a chart set to a volume of 1000 will generate a new candlestick when that amount is traded, regardless of how many trades needed to reach that volume.

The main negative aspect of using this type of chart is that we cannot use volume analysis techniques on it.

Range Charts

While the two types presented above use volume data as the basis for their representation, a range chart is based on price data.

This type of chart represents market activity from the point of view of price movement. All of its bars will be displayed with the same size, regardless of how long it took for them to appear. More bars will appear in high volatility environments, and vice versa for low volatility environments.

If the chart is set to a range of 15, new bars will appear when the price moves 15 ticks in one direction or another.

TOOLS FOR VOLUME ANALYSIS

Thanks to certain tools that analyze the flow of orders, we can see all the interaction between buyers and sellers who participate in the market in different ways.

They can be distinguished by the type of orders they deal with, since not all these tools are based on the same data:

- Analysis of pending orders: Order Book, also called Depth of Market (DOM).

- Analysis of executed orders: Tape (Time & Sales) and Footprint.

To give you a basic understanding of the peculiarities of each characteristic, below is a description of each one.

Order Book

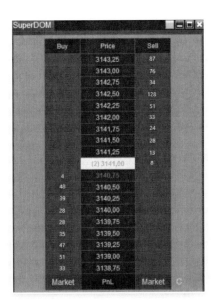

Identifies all orders pending execution (liquidity) that are located in the BID and ASK columns. As we already know, the BID represents the pending buy orders and the ASK represents the pending sell orders.

Since this type of software only offers a depth of Level 2, most markets can only show ten levels of liquidity above and below the current price. This is relevant because there will continue to be liquidity located beyond these ten levels, but it is only visible to those with a depth of Level 3 (mainly liquidity providers).

The analysis of the order book throws up some problems. One of them is that the visible liquidity is in no case the liquidity that is actually located at said levels. The liquidity that is displayed in the order book comes only from the limit orders (Limit). By their very nature, market orders cannot be observed anywhere, since they are born from a trader's initiative and are executed instantly. Meanwhile, Stop orders, which become market orders when their price is reached, are not displayed in the Order Book either.

In addition, as we have seen orders with some advanced characteristics, there are certain instructions that also prevent these from being displayed in the order book, so in reality we aren't actually analyzing a very high percentage of the total orders pending execution.

Another major problem with the analysis of the order book, or any other tool based on this liquidity data, is that pending orders can be eliminated at any time before execution, by whoever placed them. As a result of this peculiarity, different forms of algorithm manipulation emerged:

Spoofing

This is the location of huge amounts of contracts in the BID and ASK columns (limit orders) without the intention that the execution of said orders actually take place. The goal is to give the impression of an "insurmountable barrier" and cause the price to move to the opposite side. They are false orders because when the price is going to reach their level, they are canceled and are not executed.

It is an interesting concept that highlights the ability of limit orders with respect to price movement. As we have mentioned, limit orders by themselves and by their very nature do not have the capacity to move the market, but using this form of manipulative activity we see how the price can move influenced by them at certain times. Not directly based on their execution, but indirectly based on their influence.

Imagine that you normally see limit order amounts around 50 contracts per price level. What will the rest of the participants think if they suddenly see 500 contracts? Well, the most logical thing is that they see that it is a price too expensive to pay for the price to cross that level and it is most likely that a lack of interest will be caused to go against said orders. And of course this will translate into a movement in the opposite direction of the huge order. Manipulating the big traders to push the price in the direction they want.

Iceberg Orders

This is the partitioning of a large limit order into other smaller portions. The motivation to carry out this type of action has to do with wanting to hide the real size of the original order.

Mainly used by institutional traders who want to execute a huge number of contracts in a certain price range and who use algorithms programmed with this technology to be able to do it passively and without putting the price against them. It is important to note that there is only one source behind such an order, only one big trader, not a set of them.

It is very visual to take the example of a real Iceberg. On the surface, what is seen is an apparently normal number of contracts, but what is not known is that this order is simply a part of a much larger one. And that when this small part is filled by the market, the large order replenishes it quickly.

It is the clearest example of what an **absorption** would be. There may be many aggressive buyers pressing the ASK and all those Buy Markets are matching the Sell Limits of an Iceberg order which do not allow the price to move higher. We will say that an absorption of these buying is taking place.

The same would happen for the selling absorption. Sell Markets pressing on the BID column with the aim of entering aggressively short but the price does not move down because they are blocked by Buy Limits that consume all that liquidity.

Time & Sales

Thanks to Time & Sales we can see in real time all the matching orders already executed. Tape analysis is made very complex by the speed at which current markets (primarily futures markets) move.

Depending on the software we can access different types of information. It usually includes at least the columns with the time of execution, the price level and the number of contracts.

It can certainly be useful for the identification of large volumes executed in a single order, which is known as a "big trade". More modern versions also allow the grouping of orders executed by blocks, indicating the same trader as the origin of different transactions spaced out over time.

A positive point of the Tape with respect to the Order Book is that the tape represents the past, the orders already executed and therefore it is not susceptible to manipulation.

Trading solely by analyzing the tape is not within everyone's reach as it requires enormous experience in addition to having a great capacity for concentration due to the speed at which it moves.

Footprint

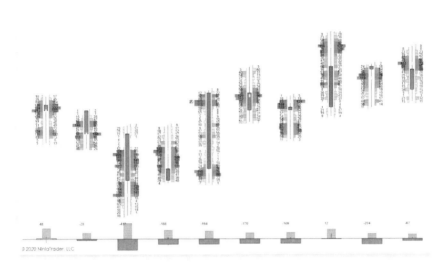

When most refer to the Order Flow, they are actually referring to this section of the order flow, to the use of the Footprint. Order Flow is a general term that, as its name suggests, has to do with the flow of orders.

The Footprint graphs the data provided by the tape (orders already executed) and represents them in a much more visual way. It would be like putting a magnifying glass inside the candlesticks and observing the number of contracts executed at each price level.

The advantage of analyzing the Footprint is that it allows us to quantify the interaction between buyers and sellers in maximum detail. Observing the balance and imbalance between the participants as well as being able to identify in which column the most volume is being traded can certainly be useful at certain times.

There are different types of footprint graphing based on:

- The nature of the data: can be configured with time, range, volume and rotation candlesticks.

- To the representation protocol: Profile, Delta, Imbalance, Histogram, Ladder or BID/ASK.

It is a highly configurable tool that generally includes multiple functionalities, although it basically analyzes the orders executed by price levels with the aim of looking for imbalances, absorptions, initiatives, unfinished auctions, clusters, big trades, etc.

Once it is known in depth how the matching orders is executed, the conclusion is reached that its analysis is very subjective and that trading based on this tool without taking anything else into account is not recommended at all.

Delta

A more specific and popular tool within the world of order flow analysis is the Delta. The delta is an indicator that simply measures the difference between the volume traded in the BID and the volume traded in the ASK in a given period of time. If the difference is positive, the delta will be positive and vice versa if it is negative. In addition, it will also be possible to visualize the difference between deltas since normally the indicators will show them with different sizes.

There is a very common mistake in thinking that all the volume traded in the ASK "are buying" and that all the volume traded in the BID "are selling", although in reality with that statement they mean that they have a directional origin ; that is, they have an intention to add pressure to one side. If this were so, why do we sometimes see bearish movements with positive deltas and bullish movements with negative deltas? Trust me it's not that simple. If so, we would have found the Holy Grail. Again it has to do with the order matching mechanism.

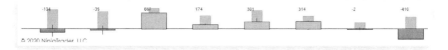
© 2020 NinjaTrader, LLC

For now, we are going to stay with the fact that it is visually observed on a horizontal axis with a value of 0 and that depending on the column where the transactions are executed, it will be visualized positively and negatively on the axis. This representation would be for the example of the normal Delta since there is another variant, the accumulated one, where it is graphed continuously without taking into account the horizontal axis.

The delta is updated in each executed order and therefore gives rise to the possibility that, as happens with the price, wicks are represented at its ends. If we observe a delta with a wick in its lower part, what it will mean to us is that at a certain moment of its development the difference in favor of the BID was extraordinarily large, and that at a certain point it has begun to negotiate much more actively in the column of the ASK generating that reversal that leaves its mark in the form of a wick.

As happens in general terms with the analysis of the trace, although its interpretation is not as basic as I have explained above, it can provide us with some utility at certain specific moments.

THE PROBLEM OF MATCHING ORDERS

As a basis, we must have a series of clear ideas that will make it easier for us to understand the rest of the content:

- A buy matches a sell and vice versa.

- An aggressive order matches a passive order.

- Only aggressiveness is reflected in the BID and ASK columns.

Taking into account the different types of orders, it is now necessary to understand what is the mechanism used to match the orders between the participants and in which column said execution is reflected.

Order type	Matches with	Appears in
Buy Market	Sell Limit	ASK
Buy Limit	Sell Market	BID
Buy Stop	Sell Limit	ASK
Buy Stop Limit	Sell Market	BID
Sell Market	Buy Limit	BID
Sell Limit	Buy Market	ASK
Sell Stop	Buy Limit	BID
Sell Stop Limit	Buy Market	ASK

- Stop orders become Market orders when they are hit.

- Stop Limit orders become Limit orders when the price set by the Stop order is reached.

When the trader executes a Buy Market order, the mechanism that processes the orders is put into trading and goes to the Order Book to find the first sell limit order (Sell Limit) that is located in the ASK column with which to marry this buy.

The same happens when executing a Sell Market order. The processing mechanism directs that order to the most immediate price level of the BID column to find the counterparty in the Buy Limits that are pending matching there.

With limit orders the process is the same. A participant leaves his order pending execution in one of the two columns and it will stay there until an aggressive trader arrives who needs to match his order.

This is essentially what happens over and over again at high speed. Regardless of the type of order used to enter the market, the end result will always be that an aggressive order will be crossed with a passive one:

Buy Market	X	Sell Limit	=	ASK
Sell Market	X	Buy Limit	=	BID

And the column on which these order crossings will be displayed will depend on the order that has initiated it. Therefore:

- Buy Market intersects with Sell Limit and is displayed in the ASK column, since the order that has initiated the transaction is the aggressive buy.

- Sell Market intersects with Buy Limit and is shown in the BID column as the initiation comes from the aggressive sell.

Now we are going to do a reasoning exercise using the example of a trader who enters the market with a short position (sell). This trader has different ways to exit said position:

- Through a manual exit, either at a loss or at a profit by executing a buy Market order (and it would appear in the ASK).

- By executing the stop loss, whose order will be a buy stop (and would appear in the ASK).

- By executing the take profit, whose order is a buy limit (and would appear in the BID).

Similarly, a trader who enters the market with a long position (buy), may leave it through three options:

- Through a manual exit, either at a loss or at a profit by executing a sell market order (and it would appear in the BID).

- By executing the stop loss whose order will be a sell stop (and would appear in the BID).

- By executing the take profit whose order will be a sell limit (and would appear in the ASK).

What is intended to convey with this example is that the same action, such as closing a position, can be displayed in different columns (BID and ASK) depending on the type of order used for it.

Understanding this information is of tremendous importance because many cross-order analyzes are flawed by starting from the wrong premises.

The first conclusion, therefore, should be that not everything that appears executed in the ASK column is a buy with the intention of adding buying pressure to the market, nor is everything that appears in the BID column a sell with the intention of adding selling pressure. Here lies the problem when analyzing the flow of orders in any of its variants.

These programs based on the mechanism of the matching orders are configured to always reflect aggressiveness, the problem is that it is not possible to distinguish what intention is behind the executed orders.

Intent of the orders executed at the BID	Intent of the orders executed at the ASK
Aggressive selling	Agressive buying
Passive buying	Passive selling
Manual closing of a buy	Manual closing of a sell
Stop Loss of a buy	Stop Loss of a sell
Take profit of a sell position	Take profit of a buy position

When we see a cross executed in the ASK, it will always be a buy market order (Buy Market) with a limited sell (Sell Limit); while when we see a cross executed in the BID, it will be a sell market order (Sell Market) with a limited buy (Buy Limit), but what we will not know is the origin/intention behind such a cross of orders:

The main source of error when facing the order flow analysis comes from the belief that everything executed in the ASK has a buying initiative and everything executed in the BID has a selling initiative, but as we have just to see, nothing is further from reality. This type of software makes a reduction to the execution of aggressive orders with passive ones, but they cannot know what is the origin/intent of those orders.

What would happen if there is a matching orders of a Stop Loss of a sell (Buy Market) and a take profit of a buy (Sell Limit)? This type of cross will be reflected in the ASK, but is there really an intention to add buying pressure to the market? Obviously not, as we see in this example, both traders would be left out of the market and yet their transaction would be reflected in the ASK. This is the problem with Order Flow: it is still a tremendously subjective tool. Even more so when it is not perfectly known how the matching orders works.

We found the same problem for the BID column. There could be the possibility of a marriage of orders from someone who has jumped the stop loss of a buying position (Sell Market) together with someone who wants to take profits from a selling position (Buy Limit). This cross would be reflected in the BID but both are out, there is no new selling pressure.

Next I am going to propose two different contexts to exemplify again the problem of the Order Flow:

Problem #1 Price Divergence

For example, if, analyzing the footprint chart, we see a bullish development in which an imbalance (green background) in favor of ASK is observed in its upper part, with a downward turn immediately afterwards; this fact offers us different interpretations.

Some would say that these are trapped buyers (assuming that ASK imbalance as aggressive buying with directional intent); others will say that they are executions of Stop Loss orders of short positions; still others will say that they are taking profits from long positions; and finally someone else may say that it is a passive entry of sellers (absorption through sell limit orders).

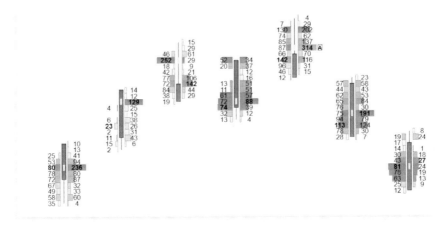

Everyone is probably correct. And the truth is that it is most likely that there is a bit of all this. Also, at that point the delta will most likely be negative, showing us a divergence.

This is where the problem becomes evident when analyzing the Order Flow. The truth is that in real time we cannot determine exactly what the true origin of these executions is. In many cases, in order to justify a proposed scenario, reference will be made to one of those reasons in particular. For example, someone who is looking for a bearish move or who is already short will see those large orders executed in the ASK and will assume them as "trapped buyers", since it is the reason that would justify their bearish approach.

The only objective in this example is that, when it appears in the ASK column, it is a cross between Buy Market and Sell Limit orders; but from there to stating categorically that it is any of the possible origins already described does not seem like a very solid approach.

Hence the importance that, in case of deciding to work with Order Flow, the most logical thing would be to subordinate its analysis to the context that another approach can provide, such as the Wyckoff methodology in our case. The why is because due to the complexity and nature of order matching we are going to find these types of imbalances anywhere on the chart and this does not offer us an advantage.

Problem #2 Delta Divergence

What happens when the Delta is not consistent with the price? In a positive Delta your candlestick is expected to be bullish; and in a negative Delta, bearish. Divergence would appear when we see a negative Delta on a bullish candlestick or a positive Delta on a bearish one.

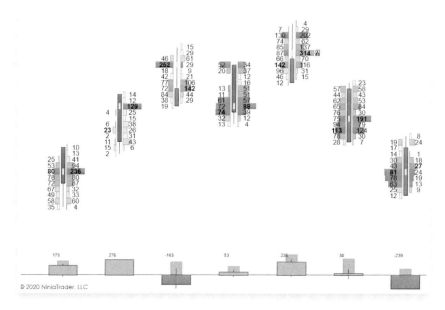

If all that appears in the ASK were market buying with the intention of adding upward pressure, it is impossible that a positive Delta would result in a bearish candlestick.

Continuing with the same example as above, we see that the bearish candlestick that causes the reversal has a very positive delta (+235).

The reasoning for this situation could be the following: The positive delta may be the result of many aggressive buying (Buy Market) that have been blocked with passive selling (Sell Limit) and have not allowed the price to rise. All that matching orders appears in the ASK. Subsequently, as there is little demand in the BID (few Buy Limits orders), a few aggressive selling now would cause the price to move downwards. And this is one way that a positive delta with a bearish candlestick would eventually be seen.

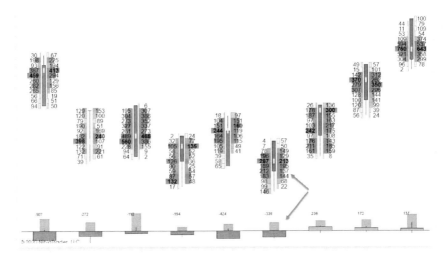

As you may have concluded, delta divergences implicitly identify an absorption so if they appear in the right place they often herald interesting turns. This does not mean far from it that all the divergences will establish turns since sometimes these will take place on an area of little interest and without that intention of absorption behind it, hence the problem of its use arbitrarily.

The Price and Volume Trader

In the end, our task as traders is to identify when imbalances between supply and demand occur and these will eventually show up on the price and volume chart.

A trader who only takes into account the price and volume action may enter the market with a certain delay in addition to not having certain information available (the real interaction between the participants) but his trading will be much calmer by not having to interpret those order crossings.

In the previous example of price divergence, the trader who simply analyzes price action and volume will only focus on the fact that there has been an anomaly in that action, an effort result divergence. This large number of executed orders will most likely be accompanied by an increase in volume and a narrow range already denoting some divergence. In addition, a subsequent turn to the downside would confirm this anomaly.

Beyond entering to assess whether what has been there is a stop jump, profit taking, entry of short positions or that buyers have been trapped; which, as we have already mentioned, is probably a bit of all of the above, what is relevant is the final action and the trader who does not observe the flow of orders but knows how to interpret the chart will eventually reach the same conclusion, albeit with less stress.

Conclusion

In addition to everything mentioned regarding the matching of orders, it is the precise moment to also remember the different types of agents that trade in the market and the intention behind their actions (hedging, speculation and arbitrage). The orders that these participants execute are also shown on the BID and ASK, and as we have seen, not all of them have directional intentions that are ultimately the ones looking for price movement.

This is no small matter as the only ones who will show up again to defend their position should they have aggressively entered the market looking to profit from the price movement will be the speculative traders. We may see the execution of a large order at a price level and that it comes from some institution with the aim of covering a position that it maintains in another parallel market, or that it is the activation of an arbitrage strategy, to name a few. possibility.

We therefore add a new layer of opacity and subjectivity. We have on the one hand that not all participants go to the market with a speculative interest; and on the other hand that the marriage of orders cannot determine the origin of said negotiation.

We therefore come to the conclusion that the use of the Order Flow independently could be totally meaningless since in no case can it offer us what is the most important aspect to determine in the market: the context; know exactly where we are going to look for trades and in which direction. Trying to understand this is vital to be able to carry out robust analysis and scenario planning.

Free gift #2: Video: Auction Market Theory

To complement the content in this second part, I'm giving you a video where I explain auction theory and how the market moves between zones of balance and imbalance in a constant cycle.

You can access from this link: https://tradingwyckoff.com/book-2/

or by scanning this QR code directly::

PART 3. VOLUME PROFILE

The Volume Profile is a variant of the Market Profile®, a tool designed by J. Peter Steidlmayer in 1985 for the Chicago Board of Trade (CBOT®).

Steidlmayer was a trader and executive member in this major futures and options market for more than 40 years. This new method of auction representation was initially intended only for CBOT members, although it quickly spread abroad. We can therefore infer that their approach to how the market moves does not seem to be on a bad basis.

Unlike the analysis of the Order Flow, the Volume Profile is totally objective since it does not require any type of interpretation and therefore it provides us with very useful information for our analyzes and scenario approaches.

With the analysis of the Volume Profile we return to treat all the concepts initially presented in the theory of the auction (Auction Market Theory). We do not focus on determining the intention of a particular order cross, but we expand the picture to identify the most relevant trading zones.

Volume Profile is not an indicator. It is simply another way of representing the volume's data. It clearly and precisely identifies the number of contracts traded at different price levels.

Auction Theory + Volume Profile

The Volume Profile uses the principles of auction theory to put it into practice and to be able to visualize the areas of interest on the chart. Interest is simply measured by the activity that has been generated in a particular area; and that activity is identified by the volume traded.

In this way, this tool can help us to identify the areas of greatest and least interest and we can use it evaluate the price that interacts with these areas, in order to determine if there is acceptance or rejection.

All of these principles are based on the premise that the market has a memory and tends to repeat behavior. Therefore, it is expected that in the future certain areas will behave in the same way as they did in the past.

One caution to keep in mind is that market memory is mostly short-term. This means that the most recent trading areas are more important than the older ones. If the price initiates an imbalance, the first zone to take into account will be the most immediate previous balance zone.

The longer the price has been away from a certain acceptance area, the less significant it will be. If we do not have another reference, it will still be useful to value it, but it is important to be aware that the most immediate balance zones will most likely be the ones that the market will look for in the first instance, since they are the ones that best represent the value at the present time.

COMPOSITION OF THE VOLUME PROFILE

Volume profiles are visually displayed on the chart as a horizontal histogram, whose values are distributed according to the traded volume of each price level.

Depending on the number of contracts that are exchanged at each price level, the shape of the distribution will vary. The more transactions, the greater the length of the horizontal line; while a short horizontal line represents fewer trades.

As a reference we are going to take a normal distribution or Gaussian Bell to understand the most important statistical concepts:

- The data is distributed symmetrically about the central point where the mean, median and mode coincide.

- It has three standard deviations on each side, which are equally spaced apart and measure the amount of variability or spread around an average. It is also a measure of volatility.

- The first standard deviation comprises 68.2% of the data and up to the second standard deviation 95.4% is reached.

Value Area (VA)

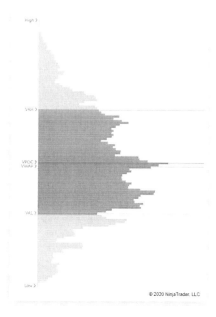

This real example has the form of a normal distribution where the values are distributed above and below around the central point.

The data is organized by means of a vertical axis in which the price is located and a horizontal axis that represents the volume variable.

The value area is determined between the Value Area High (VAH) and the Value Area Low (VAL), is part of the first standard deviation and represents exactly 68.2% of the total volume traded in that profile. It is the most traded area of the profile and therefore it is considered an acceptance area.

The volume operated outside the value area comprises the remaining 31.8%. It is the least traded zone of the profile and therefore it is considered a rejection area.

The high and low levels of the value area (VAH and VAL) will act as support and resistance areas as some interaction is expected on them.

The breadth of the value area leaves us clues about market conditions. A large Value Area suggests that there is a large participation of all traders, all are buying and selling at the prices they want; while a narrow Value Area is a sign of low activity.

Extremes

This is the highest (High) and lowest (Low) price reached in that profile. These price levels should always be viewed as key reference points.

Depending on the negotiation that is generated at these extremes, we can consider that they represent finished or unfinished auctions.

• **Auction finished**. It is visually observed with a decreasing negotiation towards the extreme. It represents a lack of interest as the price reaches price levels further away from the value area, ultimately suggesting a clear market refusal to trade in that zone. By its very nature it is a Low Volume Node.

Prices have reached a point where some traders have seen it as an advantageous opportunity and have entered causing that rejection. The lack of participation of the opposite side is represented by this decrease in volume.

• **Unfinished auction**. It appears as a zone of high trading (High Volume Node) on the end of the profile. It implicitly represents an interest in trading in said area and therefore suggests a subsequent visit of the price if it has previously moved away from it. In the future visit, the intention behind it will have to be evaluated, since it could be carried out with the aim of ending the auction and turning around, or with the aim of continuing to negotiate and continue in that direction.

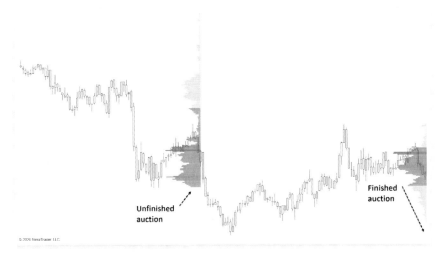

This concept of a finished or unfinished auction can be very useful since, for example, if we are assessing the possibility that the price will leave an balance zone upwards, we will want to see that in the lower part of said zone there is a finished auction that would suggest a lack of of interest to trade there. In case of observing a possible unfinished auction, it would be convenient to quarantine the scenario since it is most likely that before starting the upward movement there will be a visit of the price in that low part with the aim of testing the interest in that area.

When in doubt as to whether we are in a possible finished or unfinished auction, it is advisable to treat it as finished. Unfinished auctions should be very visual and shouldn't be shrouded in a lot of subjectivity. Generally we are going to observe them as an abnormal cut in the profile distribution and in many occasions it will coincide with one of the two Value Area limits.

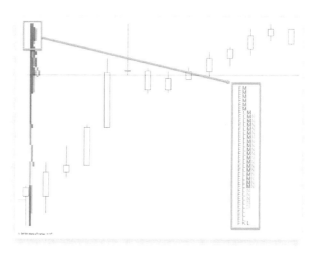

In Market Profile this concept is totally objective: an unfinished auction (Poor High & Poor Low) appears at one extreme where at least two TPOs are observed; or what is the same, a finished auction will be represented with a single TPO in the price level (Single Print).

Volume Point of Control (VPOC)

It is the level of highest volume concentration in that profile. It represents the most accepted price by both buyers and sellers (more fair) and establishes the level from which the value area is calculated.

Since most of the volume comes from large institutions, this is where these large traders have accumulated most of their positions. They generally accumulate contracts in a range of prices, but the VPOC represents a reference point since it identifies where the greatest interest is.

As it is a level that will attract many trades, it is generally advised to avoid trading in its immediate vicinity. The broad consensus among participants will cause fluctuations around that level. Behavior that will be maintained until new information appears that unbalances the perception of the participants.

The VPOC allows us to establish who has control of the market. If the price is above it, we will determine that the buyers will be in control, so it would make more sense to go long; if it is below, the sellers will have it, so going short would be a better option.

Keep in mind that the VPOC, by its very nature, will always be a High Volume Node, but not all High Volume Nodes will be VPOCs.

Volume Weighted Average Price (VWAP)

If there is a level widely used by large institutions, it is the VWAP. Huge transactions seek to be executed at the price level where the VWAP is and that is why it has raised its level of importance.

The VWAP represents the average price of all contracts traded during a specific time period. The formula for obtaining it is as follows:

No. of contracts traded * asset price / total contracts traded

To understand it a little better, we can say that above the VWAP there is the same traded volume as below it, that is, it represents an important balance level. This balance causes that when the price reaches the VWAP there are equal probabilities that the price will go up or down.

It is displayed on the chart as a traditional moving average and its position varies as the transactions are executed. Generally, depending on the trading style, the VWAP of the session, the weekly or the monthly are usually used.

The VWAP is used by institutional traders mainly as a means to determine the value of the asset at that given moment, so they consider that they have bought low if the price is below and that they have bought high if it is above.

The institutions have taken the VWAP as a reference measure with which to judge the quality of their executions, hence its relevance and that we treat it as an important trading level. When they receive an order, they do not execute all the contracts they need at once, but they will try to do it gradually knowing that their work will be judged based on that reference level.

Session VWAP
Weekly VWAP
Monthly VWAP

Because it represents an important level of balance or fair price, it is a good measure of whether we are buying too high or selling too low. We can know this by adding one or two standard deviations to the mean. That the price is in some standard deviation does not mean that it cannot continue moving in that direction, we could simply use it as one more mark to add to our analysis.

But be very careful because everything is subject to the valuation of the market at that time. In a balanced market, a price below the VWAP will be considered cheap and a price above it will be considered expensive; but just when the market is unbalanced to one side or the other, the VWAP stops representing efficiency since now the perception of value has changed.

Depending on the time frame we can make use of different VWAP levels. The most commonly used are the session VWAP for day traders and the weekly and monthly VWAP for medium and long-term traders.

High Volume Nodes (HVN)

High volume nodes. They are zones that represent balance and a high level of interest by all market participants since both buyers and sellers have been comfortable making transactions there. It is observed as peaks in the volume profile.

Although for this example we have used a Composite type profile, the fundamentals are equally valid and applicable to all profiles.

Past balance zones act like magnets attracting price and keeping it there. Since there was some consensus between buyers and sellers in the past, exactly the same is expected to happen in the future. That is why they are very interesting areas for goal setting.

Within the same profile, different High Volume Nodes can be identified.

Low Volume Nodes (LVN)

Low volume nodes. These are areas that represent imbalance/rejection. Neither buyers nor sellers have been comfortable trading and therefore prices are considered somewhat "unfair". It is observed as valleys in the volume profile.

As there was no consensus in the past, it is expected that in the future there will be no consensus either and they will cause some rejection, so they are interesting areas of support and resistance where to look for potential entries.

It is important to understand that rejection can be represented by price in two ways:

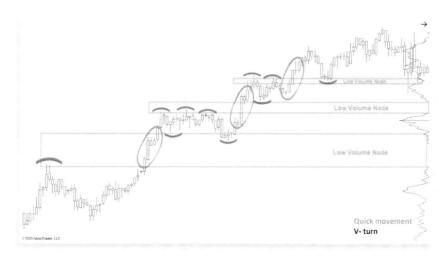

• **V-turn**. The perception of value has not changed with respect to the previous balance zone and there is a refusal to quote at said levels. The market turns completely around to re-enter the previous zone where buyers and sellers feel comfortable trading.

What causes this reaction in the price is in the first instance the placement of passive orders waiting on said zone to block the movement, together with a subsequent aggression that confirms the V-turn and return to the previous value area.

Visually it may be seen in price as prominent wicks at the ends of the candlesticks which will suggest such a rejection.

• **Fast scrolling**. The perception of value by participants has changed and is represented in the price by a violent movement. The market, based on the new information, refuses to quote at those levels of the LVN and goes through it quickly.

Technically, what causes this rapid movement is, on the one hand, the execution of protection orders (Stop Loss) of those who are positioned on the opposite side; and the activation of momentum strategies that enter aggressively with market orders.

Visually it will be observed on the chart with wide range candlesticks generally accompanied by high volume.

Like the HVNs, more than one Low Volume Node can be viewed within the same profile.

PROFILE TYPES

The volume profile is a tool that can be adapted according to the needs of the trader.

The main difference when using one type of profile or another will be determined by the trader's work schedule and the context he needs to cover in his analysis.

Basically we can differentiate between three types of profiles:

Fixed range

This type is very versatile. What makes it unique is that it allows us to manually launch profiles on any particular price action.

Especially useful for identifying trading zones in two types of contexts: trend movements and ranges.

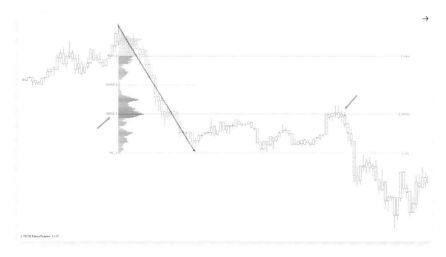

If we see a downward trend movement we can launch a profile of all the momentum to identify the interesting areas where the price is likely to make some kind of upward pullback. It is in these trading areas where we want to be prepared to evaluate the possibility of joining in favor of the trend. In the example we see how the price tests the VPOC of the downward momentum and from there a turn is generated that causes the development of a new downward movement.

If what we have is a context of lateralization, a structure that we work under the Wyckoff methodology approach, the profile will come in handy to mainly identify where the VPOC is that determines the control of the market and the value area with its extremes (VAH and VAL). These will be very interesting to take into account in order to search for the test after the structure breaks on them, as in the following example.

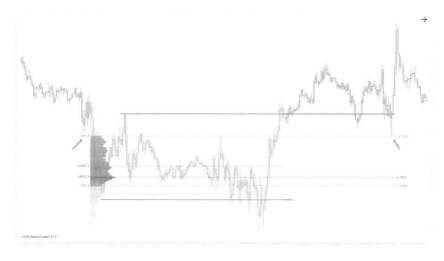

Unlike the other types of profiles, the fixed range is not updated and only analyzes the volume traded in the area that is determined.

Regardless of whether you are going to work with structures or not under the Wyckoff methodology approach, it is very useful to draw profiles that encompass several sessions in case we see an overlap between their value areas. If we see more than one session generating value over a certain price range, it is best to launch a profile that includes all the price action, since the trading levels that said profile can provide us with will, by their very nature, be more relevant.

Session

This is the profile for the day. Especially useful for intraday operations where the most important trading areas of the session are taken into account. Its range includes from the beginning to the end of the session, so it is updated as the day progresses.

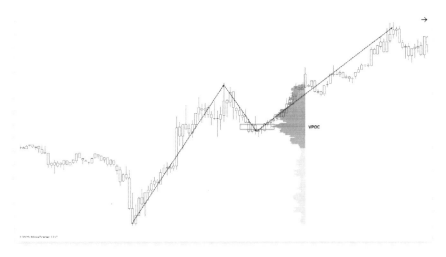

Shorter-term traders use both session levels and previous sessions to make their scenario approaches.

If we find ourselves observing an upward movement and a subsequent lateralization of the price, it would be interesting to look for the incorporation in favor of the trend movement on some trading level. As we know, the most important level of the entire profile is the VPOC, so we must take it into account to wait for our entry trigger on it.

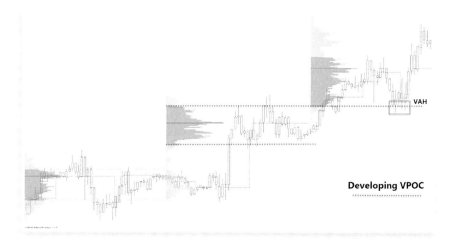

Continuing with this same example, another interesting area to look for a test after breakout could be some trading area from previous sessions. If we are above the value area of the previous session, the first trading level on which to wait for a test to look for the bullish continuation will be the Value Area High of the profile of said previous session.

Composite

Originally profiles were only viewed by sessions and this idea of grouping them was introduced by Donald L. Jones in his book "Value-Based Power Trading" in what he called "The Overlay Demand Curve". The aim was to try to eliminate the noise of short time frames and thus obtain a better understanding of the condition and context of the market.

This type of profile can be configured in two ways:

• **Fixed**. Within the fixed mode we have the possibility to select the range of dates that we want to include in the profile analysis. You may want to know the profile of last week, last month or current year, this mode is designed for this particular requirement.

• **Variable**. Characteristically, this variable mode shows the traded volume of all the price levels currently on the chart. It is important to keep this in mind, because if you move the chart, the profile will change.

The best use of this type of profile, regardless of the time frame in which we are trading, is to analyze the general context and identify the trading zones (mainly the high and low volume nodes) that we have both for above and below the current price.

These zones will serve to point out the bias of the market in a more macro context as well as for the establishment of possible zones where to look for entries and exits.

If, for example, we are working on a structure, it is very interesting to analyze the profile of the Composite to identify the High Volume Nodes of the longest term on which to establish objectives to take profits.

Another use could be to identify a large Low Volume Node in the macro context and encourage a false breakout to develop on it. We could be working on a potential cumulative structure. If, when analyzing the context, we identify an LVN relatively close to the structure, it would be interesting to take into account the possibility that the Spring that generates the imbalance of the structure may occur on it.

DIFFERENCE BETWEEN VERTICAL AND HORIZONTAL VOLUME

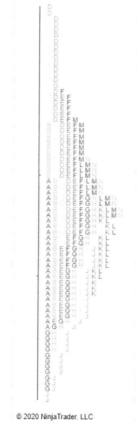

Many who view the Volume Profile with some misgiv_ings allude to the fact that it is not necessary to incor-porate this type of tools in order to be able to make solid analyzes and approaches based on the volume data.

This is totally true, it is obvious that absolutely nothing is necessary. The problem is that they fail to under-stand what kind of information they can acquire through their evaluation.

The first thing to convey is that the Volume Profile was not developed as a substitute for the classic volume. They provide different information and are therefore totally complementary.

To really understand what information the volume data provides us, it is necessary to examine it from two points of view:

•**Volume by time**: It is the classic volume that is ob_served vertically on the chart. It has to do with the number of contracts exchanged within a certain period of time. It tells us when the big traders are active.

•**Volume in price**: It is the Volume Profile and is ob_served in the form of horizontal bars. It tells us the number of contracts traded within a given price level. It informs us of where this activity of the large traders has taken place.

As we can see, both provide us with different information about the same action (professional activity), the volume by time has to do with when while the volume by price has to do with where.

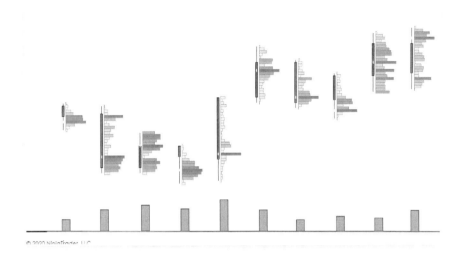

With the vertical volume we can know that during the development of a particular candlestick a specific number of contracts have been traded, but how has the trading been distributed through the different price levels?

This is the information that the horizontal volume provides us and that the classic volume cannot. Another very different matter is that you need to know this information for your operations.

Difference between Volume Profile and Market Profile

The main difference between both tools is that the Market Profile is designed based on time; while the Volume Profile is designed based on volume.

The Market Profile represents the price data on the chart in letter format, where each letter (referred to as TPO or Time Price Opportunity) identifies 30 minutes of trading. Then, the letter A will correspond to the first 30 minutes after the opening of the session, the letter B to the next 30 minutes and so on, letters and minutes will be added until the end of the day.

Traders who base their trading on Market Profile analyze the opening of the day with respect to the value area of the previous day and the evolution of the Initial Balance (range that covers the first hour of trading) to determine the type of day that is likely to happen. and propose scenarios based on it. Here it should be noted that some traders determine the Initial Balance based on the first half hour only.

Although Volume Profile traders usually do not take the Initial Balance into account, the message it conveys can be very interesting mainly because the narrower your range, the more likely there is a trending day; and the wider the range, the more likely to have a side day.

An interesting use offered by the PM is the objective determination of acceptance or rejection of a price level. While in Volume Profile this may be shrouded in subjectivity, Market Profile analysis removes this discretion: rejection is displayed by 1 TPO; while 2 or more TPOs begin to represent acceptance.

The development of the distribution of the profiles of both tools will tend to be quite similar, although it is true that they will not be exactly the same. This is obvious since they do not use the same data for their representation. An accumulation of TPOs will indicate that the price has spent a long time at that certain level; while an accumulation of volume will mean that a large number of contracts have been exchanged at that level.

In Volume Profile, being designed based on volume, the most traded level will not necessarily be the level where the most time has been spent; Well, the price may reach a level that in a few seconds accumulates a large number of orders and turns around (as in the example). The time that the price will have spent at that level is short, but the volume traded is long; so the Volume Profile POC will be at that level while the Market Profile POC will not.

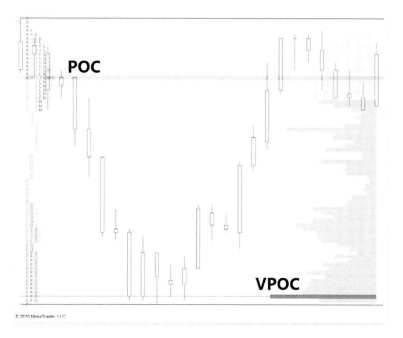

Due to the current ecosystem of financial markets where the importance of volume is evident, it would seem more interesting to use the combination of price + volume (Volume Profile) rather than price + time (Market Profile).

This does not mean that the time variable is not important or less important, nothing is further from reality. Obviously time is a key element in establishing where participants decide the value of a particular market is at a particular time. The consumption of time on a certain area is an unquestionable sign of acceptance and therefore value construction.

PROFILE SHAPES

Obviously, the market will not always develop distributions of D-shaped profiles, since this would mean that we are in an infinite balance context.

There is a lot of theory written in Market Profile about the different types of days based on the shape of the profile (normal day, normal variation, trend day, double-distribution trend day, non-trend day, neutral day, neutral day extreme).

The truth is that identifying the shape of these profiles to determine what kind of day we have had can be valid for the human mind from the point of view that we always want to control everything and we need to find a logic for each behavior; but from an trading point of view it does not seem to be a very useful approach since the categorization is done through a posteriori analysis.

In addition, evidence has been provided over time that it is not possible to consistently predict what type of day is most likely to occur based solely on the categorization of the previous day. Steidlmayer himself finally recognized this. As it could not be otherwise, it is impossible to know what form the profile of the current session will have until it has finished.

Exactly the same thing happens with the labeling of events, phases and structures under the approach of the Wyckoff methodology. It can be useful for beginners to feed the subconscious with the different ways in which the market can represent accumulations and distributions; but it is totally useless from the trading point of view since the confirmation of all this is done a posteriori.

It would seem more sensible therefore, in order to propose trading scenarios, to focus on the identification of the creation of a value area (range) and to evaluate the price continuously by interacting at its extremes in order to identify acceptance or rejection. The analytical tools offered by the Wyckoff methodology help us determine who is more likely to be in control during the development of the range (buyers or sellers) and therefore in which direction the path of least resistance lies.

During the development of the movements, the profiles will be generated and two very common forms in which the trend and lateralization behavior are graphically observed are the b and P patterns.

These patterns represent the first three phases of market activity that Steidlmayer presented in his early studies and that by Wyckoff methodology we identify as Phases A and B of structure development.

These patterns will alert us to the stop of the previous trend movement as well as the new sideways context. These two types of profiles show the same behavior but in both directions. In the first place, in the low price zone, the price moves with some fluidity, developing the trend movement until it finds traders willing to trade in the opposite direction. At that point, an balance range begins to develop, a zone of high participation that generates the bell of the profile.

As long as the price is during the trend movement we should only be looking to trade in that direction. For this we can support the VPOC in development and the rest of the trading levels.

P-Type Profile

Characteristic of upward trend movements and representative of future distribution and reaccumulation structures.

This type of profile suggests strength on the part of buyers who have been able to push the price up relatively easily until reaching a point where sellers begin to appear.

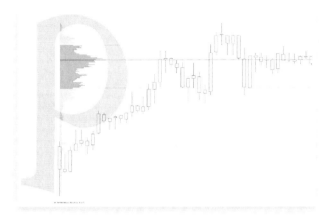

It is made up of two parts: a first where the upward imbalance is observed and a second where the market begins a rotation process (range). This is important to keep in mind because if such a process occurs in reverse (first a rotation and then a downward trend) visually we will continue to see a P-type profile with the great difference that it will have difficult trading validity.

All the concepts and tools that are being proposed have an trading meaning; and in the case at hand with the P and b patterns, they are only interesting if the last action of the price is the creation of new value (range) since it will be from there that the next exploitable imbalance will be generated. That is, if we find ourselves at the end of the move down to the point where we have already fully identified the mirrored P pattern (with the imbalance to the right), from the point of view of trading that imbalance we may be too late and it is most likely that the price will generate a new zone of balance as a more immediate action. On the contrary, if we have a theoretical P pattern (with the imbalance to the left) we will be in a position to take advantage of the subsequent trend movement (which may be upwards or downwards).

In addition to seeing it in isolation (session profiles), it is interesting to know that a longer-term uptrend will be made up of several of these profiles in its internal development. In this case, they will simply be reaccumulative structures that cause the continuous development to the upside.

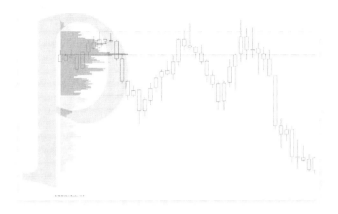

Should this type of profile appear after a prolonged downtrend, it could alert us to the imminent end of it, at least temporarily. Here it is important to note again that it refers to seeing the theoretical P pattern; since if what we see is a mirror P pattern, what we would actually have would be a distribution and therefore the downward trend would denote strength.

B-Type Profile

Characteristic of downward trend movements and representative of future cumulative and redistribution structures.

Individually, this type of profile indicates an imbalance in favor of sellers. These are in control and have strongly pushed the price down until finally some participants appear buying and a new rotation process is generated.

Within the context of a longer-term downtrend, they will appear redistributive in nature and are excellent areas to look for incorporation into the trend.

As with the P pattern, the theoretical type b is formed by a bearish imbalance as the first part and value creation as the second. A rotation first and a subsequent imbalance to the upside would also appear visually with a b-shaped profile but operationally we may not be in a position to take advantage of that first imbalance. On the other hand, it would not have the same implications when analyzing the health of the previous uptrend, where what is sought is the upward rejection and the generation of value below.

In case of observing a b-shaped profile after a prolonged upward movement, it could signal the end of said movement and sometimes the beginning of a new one towards the bearish side.

VOLUME PROFILE USES

This tool provides us with completely objective information that fits perfectly within the context provided by the principles of the Wyckoff method.

Below is a description of some of its most important uses:

Identifying Structures

There will be occasions where the delimitation of the extremes of the structures will not be very visual, possibly because the price action has generated unclean movements. In this context, it can be very useful to use the Volume Profile to indicate the high and low zones of the value area (VAH and VAL), assuming said area as the range that is generating the cause of the subsequent movement.

By their very nature, the upper and lower limits of the structures that we work with according to the Wyckoff methodology will always be low trading zones (LVN). The price turns that generate the creation of these supports and resistances are areas where the price has not wanted to negotiate and therefore they are identified as rejection. We already know that rejection is displayed within the volume profile as an LVN.

Also, on some occasions the natural ends of the structures (Creek and Ice) will coincide with the ends of the value area (VAH and VAL). By drawing a profile of that structure we can see how all the price action contained within the range will be part of the value area.

As seen in the chart below, the stop on the move up does not show very clear price action where the stop events are genuinely displayed. If we are in the final part of the development of said structure, we could draw a profile of all of it to identify the key levels by Volume Profile. In this case we see how, after the final false breakout up, the price quickly crosses the entire value area, including the VPOC and the VWAP. At that point we should be favoring the distribution and therefore the first short scenario would be to wait for the test after breakout (LPSY) on one of the trading levels. The first of these levels to take into account would be the Value Area Low since it is the first that the market would find. We see how he did this test to continue the downward development from there. The next and last level on which to look for potential LPSY would be the VPOC of the profile.

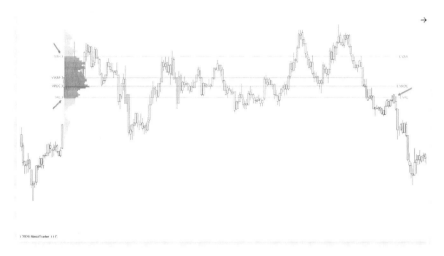

Something similar happens in this other example. Stop events may not be the most visual, plus it adds to the difficulty of framing that bull move that leaves the value area and then re-enters. The objective is that, if we find ourselves seeing an imbalance after the development of a structure already with a certain maturity, we can launch a profile to identify the trading levels on which we expect the price to develop the test looking for the continuation of the movement. Once again we see how, after the breakout movement, the test does it right on the edge of the value area of the profile, in this case on the Value Area High; is the perfect area for long entry trigger pursuits.

The **scope of the profile** should include all price action from the start of the rotation to just before the imbalance occurs. There are traders that may also include the breakout action within the profile, which is not to say that it is wrong. The only thing to keep in mind is that from an trading point of view, what we are looking for is that this test after a breakout will look for some trading level of the previous accumulation/distribution and this would leave out both the imbalance and the subsequent movement until the test.

As we can see, most of the structures that markets develop in real time are not as genuine as they are shown in the ideal examples of the book, in addition to the fact that they are all different from each other. But this does not mean that they are not operable. This is where the levels provided by the Volume Profile tool are valued.

Determining the Market Bias

Through the analysis of trading zones

We will always favor trading in the direction of the last high trading node that was generated. And a scenario against this direction would only be considered when the price has broken the area that supported the last movement.

If the price is above a high volume node (HVN) we will determine that the buyers have control and we will only propose a short scenario when the price crosses said zone below, which will suggest that the control has changed to sellers favor.

The logic is that in these nodes the price returns to an balance state and we will not be able to determine which direction it will move later. Only after confirming the effective breakout of said area would we be in a position to propose a scenario with a certain robustness.

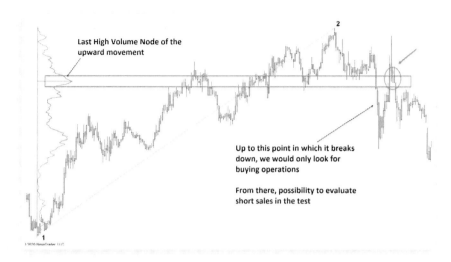

Last High Volume Node of the upward movement

2

Up to this point in which it breaks down, we would only look for buying operations

From there, possibility to evaluate short sales in the test

1

This concept is very clearly seen in the chart above. If we are in the final part of the upward movement, above the last HVN, we will have to wait for the breakout of it before looking for any short trading. The profile has been drawn covering only the upward movement (from 1 to 2), since what we are interested in knowing is where the volume node supporting said movement is located. When this is crossed down we can suggest that the control has become in favor of the bears and now we are in a position to propose a short scenario for example to the test of said HVN.

In this other example we have the same dynamic but in reverse. We spot the HVN of the bearish move in place and the idea is to continue to favor shorts until it is broken. Be careful, not until this HVN is broken, but the last one to have been generated. In other words, if the trend continues its course downwards, we will have to continue updating the profile to identify where the last HVN is and only at the moment of its upward breakout could long entry be considered.

At this point you are already
effectively positioned at the top

Last High Volume Node of the
downward movement

Possibility to search
for a buy in the test

© 2020 NinjaTrader, LLC

It should be noted that not necessarily the HVN that determines the movement control must also be the VPOC of the profile. We will simply take into account the last to develop, regardless of whether it is the VPOC or not.

Through the analysis of trading levels

As a general rule, it is best to trade with the more trading levels in your favor, the better. That is, if I am longing a trade idea, I will want to have all trading levels below the price and vice versa if I am shorting an idea. This context will suggest to us that the market is unbalanced in that direction and that it is therefore the path of least resistance.

If, in addition to this, we have the possibility of evaluating the relation-ship between the VPOC, the VWAP and the price, it will be one more mark that will add strength to the analysis.

A relatively close VWAP and VPOC is a sign that confirms the total **balance** of the market. Price is likely to be in an extremely tight range and the only trading approach here would be to look for a reversal at the ex-tremes.

This is exactly what happens on this day. The dark dotted line is the VPOC of the running session and the orange dynamic line corresponds to the VWAP. Until a final imbalance occurs below, both levels remain relatively close and this generates constant fluctuations between them, causing a range day.

To determine an **imbalance** in favor of the buyers we want to see that the price is above both the VWAP and the VPOC; while for the seller's control we want to see price below both levels.

In this chart we see an example of clear bearish control where at all times of the session the price is below both the VWAP and the VPOC, this in turn acting as resistance to originate new downward movements.

The timing to be used at these trading levels, like everything else, will depend on the trader. For an intraday trader, it is best to use the levels of the previous session and the current session. Longer-term traders may find it more useful to use such levels on a weekly timeframe (weekly VPOC and weekly VWAP). Particularly and being a structure trader, I find it useful to take into account the weekly VWAP in conjunction with the VPOC of the structure, thus eliminating temporality. It's a matter of taste and this setting should suit each trader's trading style.

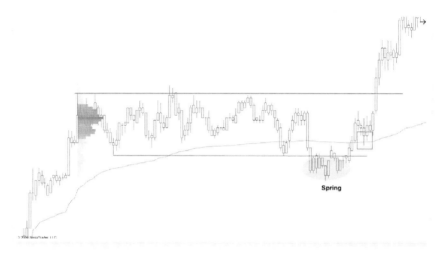

In this chart in which we are analyzing a structure, we could take a profile of it and add the weekly VWAP (green dynamic line).

It is a very good example to highlight the importance of the context above any other element.

If we see a potential Spring that manages to position itself above the VWAP, we would already be ready to look for a long entry. But if we look closely, the VPOC of the profile would still be against the VWAP that is marked in that test. We are suggesting the possibility of trading in favor of as many trading levels as possible, what do we do then? Context should prevail in cases like this. We know that the VPOC is a very important balance level, but we also know that the market will initiate an imbalance sooner or later; and that false breakout from below suggests the potential start of such an imbalance from the top. In such a context we should assign greater relevance to the development of the structure above the VPOC.

We would have done a very different reasoning if the price behind the potential Spring had not even had the ability to be above the VWAP. That lack of strength would have suggested some bearish control and one might even have valued an entry in the opposite direction seeing Spring's labeled move as a genuine bearish breakout event. Every action must be confirmed or rejected with subsequent price action.

It is just what we have in this example. In a potential Spring situation, the price tries to re-enter the range but is unable to position itself above the extreme of the structure, the VAL of the profile and the weekly VWAP. It is a sign of important weakness that would dispose us to treat such a scheme as distributive.

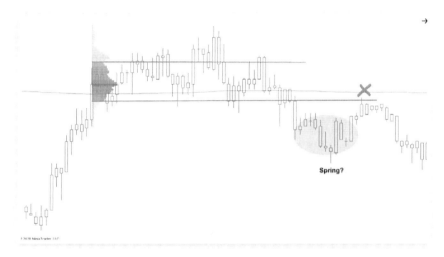

When working with different levels, it is also important to bear in mind that we can use several time frames together, for example, two VWAPs in weekly and monthly time frames. This configuration is really interesting if we decide to analyze a longer term context.

Analyzing the Health of the Trend

A very interesting trace provided by the Volume Profile is the continuous analysis of the session profile. When we are observing an upward trend movement, a health symptom of the movement would be to observe that the value areas (and therefore the VPOCs) of the sessions are generated higher and higher. What it suggests to us is that the value of the asset is being accepted in the new negotiation zones that it is reaching and therefore the trend is most likely to continue. In this context of control by buyers we should be looking for some pullback to trading zones predisposed to enter longs.

The same thing happens with downtrends. An unmistakable sign of its health would be to see that the value areas left by the sessions are observed at lower levels each time, denoting acceptance of the price. In this bearish control scenario, it is best to identify areas of potential resistance to look for incorporation in shorts.

Something that would alert us to the health of this movement would be to observe an overlap between several value areas as well as to see that some of them move against the direction of the trend, losing the dynamics that it brought. We would already be observing a consolidation of the price and it could alert us of a change in character. Using the Wyckoff methodology, we could surely already identify a lateralization process and it would be interesting to start analyzing the traces of said structure with the aim of trying to determine in which direction the next imbalance will occur.

This potential change in the perception of value is visualized very clearly with the patterns P and b. If the market is in the middle of a downtrend leaving the value zones lower and lower and suddenly a bP pattern appears, we could be facing the end of said downward movement or at least a temporary stop. The fact that the market has developed that pattern P after b suggests a change in the perception of value. At least temporarily, there is no longer any desire to trade at lower prices and we could even be facing the beginning of an upward trend.

Rather than seeking to clearly observe the ideal pattern, what is interesting is the evolution of value generation, that is, the rotation of the Value Areas. In this example, the participants have had sufficient capacity to generate value above the previous one and this alone should alert us to the health of the bearish movement and even alert us to a possible accumulation.

The same would happen in reverse. If we are looking for a bearish turn in the market, a signal that would add strength to such an analysis would be to watch a Pb pattern.

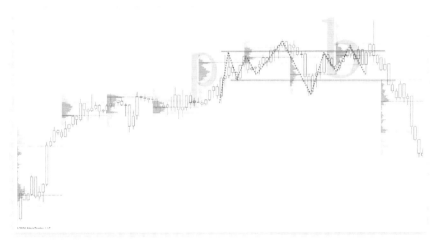

This example is a bit more complex and interesting to analyze. The first thing that draws attention is that the pattern does not occur jointly, but two sessions follow each other. On the other hand, we see how profile b does not generate value below the Value Area of profile P. This is a real example, the market behaves erratically most of the time, so looking for the appearance of perfect patterns can arrive to be a waste of time. It would seem more interesting to stay with the dynamics that exist within them; what they implicitly suggest to us.

After the appearance of the P-type profile, a change in character occurs and the market begins a rotation process. The two subsequent days the value areas are overlapping evidencing the acceptance at these price levels by the vast majority of participants. Finally, the creation of the type b profile triggers the bearish imbalance. At that precise moment when the price is below the value area of profile b and after seeing everything previously analyzed, a short scenario could be considered looking for the effect of that potential distribution structure.

If we look carefully at b, the imbalance does not occur at the beginning of the session either, as the theory suggests, but rather occurs in the last part of the day. The key is that this imbalance is rejected and re-enters the value area. In essence this is the implication behind the pattern: it doesn't matter when the imbalance occurs as long as the price generates a rejection and re-enters the value area. For trading purposes, what would be less interesting for us would be to observe the imbalance at the end of the session and whose closing is established outside the value area.

Although the ideal in potential distributive structures would be to observe in the first place that refusal to continue increasing the generation of value below the previous sessions, the appearance of this protocol in reverse (first the generation of value below and then the rejection to trade at higher prices) implicitly suggests the same reading of change in the perception of value.

In the end, all cumulative and distributive structures implicitly carry this change in the perception of value; and to a greater or lesser extent these turning patterns P and b will always be displayed.

• A bearish turn with a Pb pattern is nothing more than a distribution that will have a greater or lesser duration which has been confirmed with the generation of value in b and it is possible that lower prices will follow.

• A bullish bP pattern tacitly is an accumulation whose change in value perception possibly originates in higher prices.

VPOC Migration

The current level of the VPOC represents agreement by both parties on the value of the asset, but what reading should be done in the event of a migration of the VPOC?

This issue has brought many traders upside down since the reading it offers has two different points of view. On the one hand, many advocate that it is an unequivocal sign of the health of the movement and that it therefore suggests continuity in the direction of the trend. Many others take the position that a turnaround in the market is possible.

The only objective is that it represents a value area where the price has been accepted due to the high negotiation it has generated. The question would be to determine what sense this migration of value has, whether as continuity or as reversal.

Under the principle that each market action must be confirmed or rejected by its subsequent reaction, the key lies in evaluating the subsequent price action after the checkpoint migration. As a general rule, if we don't see a continuation in the direction of the preceding move without consuming too much time, we should question the health of that move.

Strategy with VPOC migrations

Since we can't know in advance whether a VPOC migration will make sense to continue or rollback, it's most helpful to be prepared for both scenarios. For this we are going to develop two simple protocols with the aim of establishing general guidelines.

This section is focused on intraday operations, although the underlying idea is equally valid to apply to any other time frame.

Protocol to favor reversal:

1. **The migration of the VPOC**. If the preceding trend move is healthy, after the VPOC migration we want to see new momentum develop without consuming too much time.

2. **The non-continuity**. If, after the migration of the VPOC, the price does not have the capacity to continue moving in the direction of the previous trend, we would be in a position to at least begin to question the continuity of the movement.

3. **Time consumption**. This is a fundamental sign. The general rule of thumb is that the longer the price goes by without continuing in favor of the preceding trend movement after the VPOC migration, the more likely it is that there will be a market reversal rather than a continuation.

   If we want to look for the turn, we will mainly observe that it begins to lateralize, consuming a relatively large amount of time in relation to what it had been doing previously during the continuations.

4. **Change of character.** If migration occurs, an excessive lateraliza- tion without the ability to continue in the direction it had and now an impulsive movement appears in the opposite direction, we will be in a position to propose an trading idea in reversal.

5. **Trading scenario**. The first trading level that we will consider to wait for the price and look for the entry trigger will be the end of the broken value area. If it breaks below we will wait at the VAL and if it breaks above at the VAH. As a second level, the VPOC.

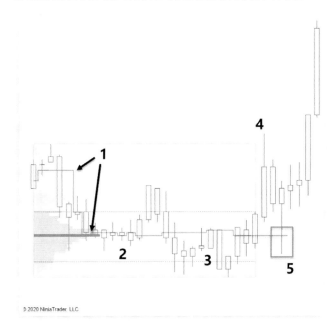

In this example (Intraday reversal trade with pattern b) a manual profile has been drawn to see how the volume was distributed at that particular moment. We see that after starting the session the price falls and the VPOC (1) migrates, later it begins to rotate on it, evidencing the non-continuity (2) and the time consumption (3). Then there is the change of character with the upward imbalance (4) to finally go to test the old VPOC area (5), where we could be looking for the long entry.

We must bear in mind that if we are trading with the profile of a session in progress, it will continue to develop as the day progresses, so after the breakout, we may identify the level of the Value Area where we are going to wait for the price and subsequently change Location. Although it is true that it would not be the ideal context, the same trading zone could be maintained since from a logical point of view this is still a low volume node and therefore an interesting zone of potential price rejection. In addition, what the price is going to test is the previous accumulation/distribution zone, so leaving the range profile is totally recommended.

In this example we see what would be a migration of the VPOC with a reversal direction (we know this after seeing the subsequent movement) but that does not follow the proposed protocol. When they do it with this urgency, with little preparation, it is practically impossible to trade. It is the problem of these V-turns.

The addition of the following example example is intended to point out that not all rollback migrations will follow the proposed protocol, far from it. With this series of steps, what we are trying to do is objectify the turn and that it is based on the Law of Cause and Effect, since once again this protocol does not stop being cumulative/distributive processes.

In addition, it is a very interesting chart to deal with the concept of acceptance and rejection. By definition, a migration of the VPOC suggests a new acceptance at these price levels. The objective fact at that precise moment is that more contracts have been negotiated (more acceptance) and therefore the migration has taken place. But what reading would you leave if it generates a complete reversal of the movement? Again, objectively, what we see is that if the session finally closes far from these levels, this action remains a rejection, even though this migration has occurred.

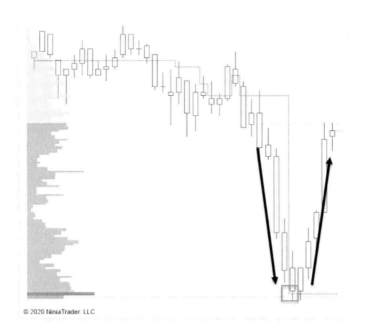

The importance of the principle that all price action must be confirmed or rejected by subsequent action appears again. In this case, the first action has been the migration of the VPOC, but this change in value has been rejected by the subsequent reaction, which has reversed the entire movement.

If we remember, a change in the perception of value occurs when the variables Price, Time and Volume work in harmony. In this case we have the Price discovery movement, the Volume generation but the Time consumption that would confirm the Value fails.

<u>Protocol to favor the continuation:</u>

For intraday continuation trading, the action protocol is much simpler:

1. **VPOC Migration**. Generally, when the market intends to continue in the direction of the previous movement, after the migration of the VPOC, the price will start the new impulse with some speed. The urgency to continue moving in that direction will cause relatively little time to be consumed before continuing in that direction.

2. **Trigger Search**. We are therefore prepared to enter the market. It is simply a matter of waiting for our configuration to appear to enter.

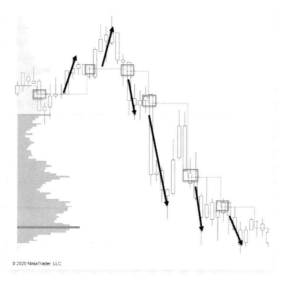

© 2020 NinjaTrader LLC

In the example we see that in the third migration of the VPOC the price, instead of continuing upwards, reverts downwards, leaving that price action on the left as distributive. From there the subsequent migrations have a sense of continuation as they are followed by bearish impulses relatively quickly.

Although this type of trading has been presented intraday, during the development of a session; they can appear on the chart in different time frames and the underlying idea will remain the same. It may develop over the course of an individual session, form over more than one session, or even develop into a longer-term structure. Regardless of its duration, the underlying logic is exactly the same.

Calibrating the Position Management

The levels to use will depend on the type of profile used based on your trading style, but in general the logic will be exactly the same for all of them:

- **Entry**. Regardless of whether we are in a trend or range context, the identification of the trading levels, mainly the VWAP, VPOC and high and low zones of the value area (VAH and VAL) will be tremendously useful to us to wait on them for the development of our market entry trigger.

- **Stop Loss**. For the establishment of the stop loss we want to identify areas where a rejection has previously occurred; and these are the low trading zones or Low Volume Nodes. The price generated a turn on them and we expect them to behave in the same way in the future, therefore it is an excellent area to place our protective stop. Aside from LVNs, the more trading levels we have going for it, the better.

- **Take Profit**. For the establishment of profit taking we are going to look for areas of high previous negotiation. As we have already discussed, High Volume Nodes (HVN) produce a certain price magnetism and therefore are excellent areas for target placement.

VALUE AREAS TRADING PRINCIPLES

Regardless of the type of trader you decide to be and therefore the time frame and structures to use, these principles are universal with respect to the value zones of a certain profile, be it that of a candlestick, session, movement or structure.

Range Principle

If the price is inside a value area, while the market condition does not change, the market will continue to generate value around the central point, so the price will most likely be rejected when reaching the extremes. Buy low and sell high.

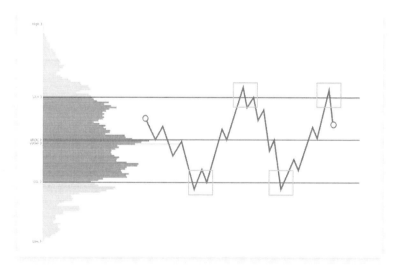

The following chart shows a real example of the principle of range trading. It can be any asset or temporary; what we do have to take into account is a reference profile on which to work. For an intraday approach, it is recommended to do it on the profile of the previous session. For longer-term approaches, weekly profiles or Composite-type profiles that include more price action may be helpful.

The interesting thing in this case is that the price is within the value area of the previous day, suggesting a balance in the market. With this basic idea, and as long as the sentiment of the participants does not change, any trading idea should go through waiting for the reversal at the extremes of its value area, as seen on the chart.

The minimum objective of this extreme reversal is a test of the control zone (VPOC), the most ambitious objective being a movement that completely traverses the value area and reaches the opposite extreme.

As always, the operations that will offer us the most confidence will be those whose trigger is located at the confluence on more than one trading level. In the example of the reversal that occurs on the VAL we see that the price also performs a test on the weekly VWAP (green line) and an old control zone (DevelopingVPOC).

Reversal Principle

If price attempts to enter a value area and succeeds, it will most likely visit the opposite end of that value area. The market has refused to trade at those price levels, so it returns to the previous value area. Adaptation of the 80% rule of Market Profile.

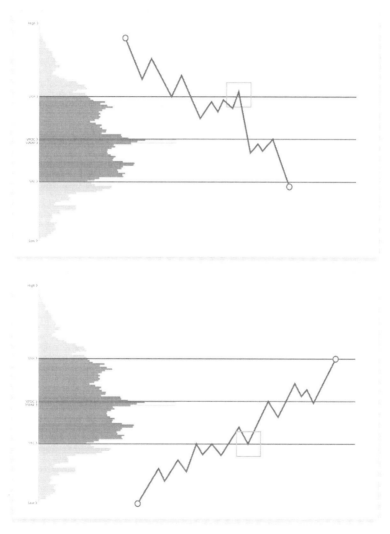

The following chart shows the opening of the last session away from the value area of the previous day at its top, indicating an imbalance to the upside and therefore initially suggesting a buying control. This control must be confirmed by accepting the imbalance and we see how the moment of truth has arrived, in a position of potential bullish continuation on the High Value Area, the price fails, re-entering the previous value area again.

It is a very instructive example to visualize the importance of having in mind both buying and selling scenarios with the aim of being prepared and reacting in time when the market tells us so. Initially in this case we would be looking for such a bullish continuation on the upper end of the value area; but seeing its inability and subsequent re-entry, the reading now is that this bullish price discovery has not been accepted and therefore the probability now is that the price will visit the opposite end of said value area.

After the initial re-entry, there is an inside test on the VAH at the confluence with the weekly VWAP (green line) to start from there the downward movement that runs through the entire value area. At that point, the price is once again in a condition of total balance, evidenced by this continuous rebound between the extremes of the Value Area.

Continuation Principle

If price attempts to enter a value area and fails to do so by being rejected at the VA end or elsewhere, it will most likely start an imbalance in that direction.

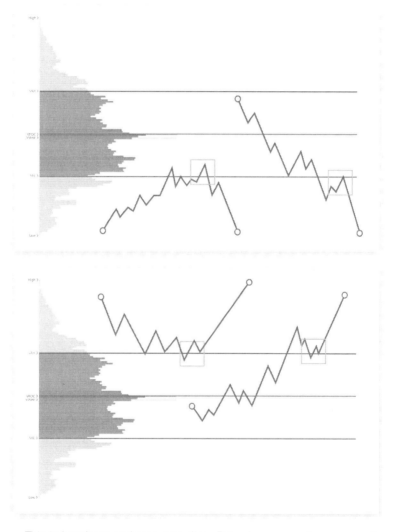

This is breakout and retest trading. Price leaves a value area and generates acceptance. This acceptance puts the direction in favor of the previous breakout as the most likely direction.

Keep in mind that the price can come from outside that value area or from within. The trading logic would be exactly the same.

In the following example we see on a real chart the development of this continuation trading principle in its variant in which the price comes from outside the working profile.

The opening occurs above the Value Area High of the profile, so the first interpretation we must make is that there has been an upward imbalance in which the buyers have had sufficient capacity to move the price away from its last value. With this basic reasoning in which the market seems to indicate that the buyers have control, the first scenario approach would be to wait for some type of test before continuing with the development in favor of the imbalance, in this case upwards.

The price opens the day and develops a certain lateralization to later go looking for the VAH area where it generates the upward turn that could offer us a buying opportunity. The most astute Wyckoff traders will be able to identify even a reaccumulative scheme from the beginning of said session, acting as a potential Spring test of said structure. It is a very good example to visualize the importance of context: in trading buying areas we want to see potential accumulations, as is the case here.

Failed Reversal Principle

If the price attempts to enter a value area and succeeds, but is strongly rejected at the VPOC of that range, the reversal trade would be nullified until further price action is seen.

If it manages to recover the end of the value area, the continuation trading would be activated; while if it finally effectively breaks the VPOC, the reversal scenario would continue to be active with the aim of going to test the opposite end of the value area.

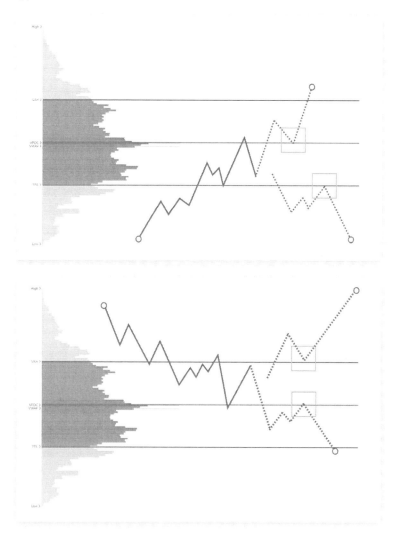

The session opens below the previous value area, so the first reasoning would be that the market is in imbalance and potential bearish control would need to be confirmed.

In the first zone on which to wait for said confirmation of the seller's control (Value Area Low), the price cancels the scenario and re-enters the value area, activating the reversal trading. As we will see later, any trading should be managed upon reaching the first relevant trading level; and in this case, a potential buy on the VAL should necessarily be managed on the VPOC of the previous session.

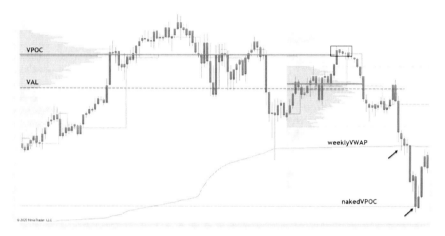

After reaching this level sellers appear unbalancing the market again and causing the development of a strong bearish movement. This aggressive reaction pushes price back out of the value area, changing market sentiment again and triggering the failed reversal plus bearish continuation trade variant at that point.

Now it does develop a successful test on the Value Area Low to start from there the bearish movement with possible targets in the weekly VWAP and in a nakedVPOC below.

Summary of the Principles of Trading Value Areas.

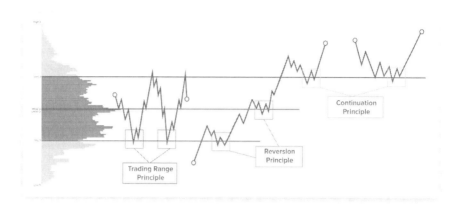

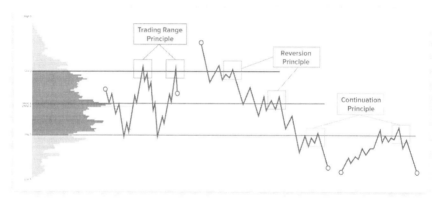

Free gift #3: Videos:

Volume Profile Basics.

Trend Health Analysis.

To complement the content in this part, I'm giving you two videos where I explain the fundamentals of Volume Profile and how to use this tool to analyze trends and identify potential price reversals.

You can access from this link: https://tradingwyckoff.com/book-2/

or by scanning this QR code directly::

PART 4. ORDER FLOW

O nce we know in depth the subjectivity involved in the analysis of the flow of orders, we come to the moment to continue reasoning to see if its use is really useful.

In general, the only time it would be useful to put the magnifying glass on the chart and look inside the candlesticks to analyze the order flow would be when the price reaches the trading zones where we are looking for the imbalances that we expect to enter the trade. market (everything depends on the context).

Being aware that the matching of orders has different intentions behind it, what we look for in these imbalances is the entry of large traders with the intention of taking risk, of speculating, of opening positions in favor of one direction or another. We will never know for sure if what we are really observing are directional orders and that is why we must limit the use of this tool only to key trading areas.

As we have already seen, the fingerprint analysis can be done in different ways based on the representation protocol. I particularly find it more visual to look at the chart using a setting known as the Volume Ladder. This type of trace allows you to observe the number of contracts executed in the different columns (BID x ASK) at the same time that it makes a representation of the volume traded at each price level within the candlestick in the form of a histogram.

The first thing to be clear about is that the order flow is read diagonally and not horizontally. This is so due to the very nature of the market in which participants can trade in different ways.

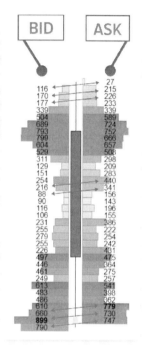

Buyers can participate either passively by leaving their demands at the BID or actively by attacking the ASK. Sellers can enter either by placing their bids on the ASK or attacking the BID with market orders.

The participants therefore have two prices with which to trade: the BID and the ASK. There is no single price at which all participants can negotiate at the same time. If so, it would make more sense to analyze the footprint horizontally instead of diagonally.

That is why, in order to assess the strength or weakness between market participants at a given price level, we will always compare executed orders diagonally upward: a BID level with respect to a higher level in the ASK column.

IMBALANCES

Many of the key actions that order flow analysis tries to identify are related to imbalances. This behavior involves a high volume of trades (high number of traded contracts) in one of the columns and at the same time a low volume of trades in the opposite column (diagonally).

It must be taken into account that this imbalance should meet minimum parameters to determine it as such. The fact that there simply appears to be a larger volume than that of the opposite column is not enough, there needs to be a disproportionate difference in volume. And this difference can be parameterized by configuring the platform to show said imbalances when a disparity of 200%, 300% or 400% appears between the levels to be compared. This will mean that on a column 2, 3 or 4 times more have been negotiated with respect to the opposite column.

Many traders also add a minimum number of contracts to gauge the imbalance. If you have a deep understanding of the market you are working in, this filter will help you refine the identification of such imbalances even further.

The fact of using these rotations in percentages allows the analysis to better adapt to market conditions and gives us some confidence since they are objective values.

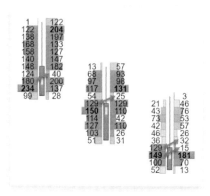

In this example chart we see imbalances in favor of the BID with a difference of 400%; or what is the same, 4 times more contracts have been negotiated in the BID than in the ASK in relation to the diagonally opposite level.

The analysis to detect possible imbalances is carried out by nature in comparative terms for two reasons:

- Because it takes into account the level of the opposite column to determine that there really is an imbalance.

- Because it will depend on the volume traded on that particular candlestick. If such an action had happened at another time (where a higher volume would have been traded in general) it might not have been seen as such an imbalance.

TURN PATTERN

Order flow analysis involves many concepts. In an attempt to simplify and try to objectify its reading, and since we are only going to analyze it in potential trading situations, we are going to be looking for the events that suggest an effective turn of the market: potential absorption and initiative.

Absorption

This is a block on the price using limit orders. There are big traders who don't want the price to move further in that direction and initially enter through passive orders to stop the move. The interesting thing is to see that after this high negotiation the price has little or no movement in that direction. Sometimes these processes will take longer and large traders will be forced to carry out such an action repeatedly during a price range, visualizing the possible absorption on more than one footprint.

When determining a possible absorption initially we want to see that it appears with a relatively high volume. This data will minimize the possibility that we are at the wrong moment in the market in which such an action is not really taking place.

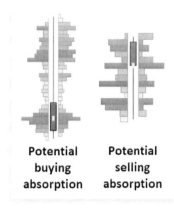

Potential buying absorption   **Potential selling absorption**

On the other hand, although the color of the candlestick is indifferent, its closing price must be against the imbalance. To treat such behavior as potential buying absorption we want to see imbalances remain above the closing price; and below the closing price for the example of potential selling absorption. It is the greatest demonstration of blocking and refusal to continue advancing in that direction.

As with any other market action, this one is confirmed or rejected by the subsequent reaction. If we see high volume, a potential takeover, and the price's inability to continue moving in that direction, the odds that we are actually looking at a takeover increase.

Although these absorptions may appear leaving wicks, it is not a necessary characteristic since they can also appear on candlesticks that close at that same end. The key there is to see that subsequently the price does not continue in that direction.

Initiative

As we have already mentioned, the execution of passive orders alone does not have the capacity to move the price, it requires aggressiveness. If the analysis is correct and we are in the right place, after seeing a possible absorption, the appearance of initiative now will be the definitive signal to confirm the market turn we were looking for.

This initiative is represented as large trades executed with market orders on the column in which we seek to enter the market: If we want to buy we will look for aggression in the ASK column and if we want to sell we will look for aggression in the BID.

Potential initiative buying

Potential initiative selling

We quote again the principle that any action must be confirmed or rejected by the subsequent reaction of the market. If we see a possible move that is followed by a subsequent immediate price move in that direction, we will be in a position to confirm such an action.

This initiative, this large volume executed, will be very easy to identify on the trace, since the imbalance with respect to the rest of the levels of the same period will be very evident. Some authors use this term to refer to several imbalances together. Although it is true that the more imbalances we observe, the stronger the approach will be; The configuration of the imbalance greatly influences its representation, since it is not the same to configure the software to show imbalances of 400% than 150%, where the latter will appear much more frequently.

As with absorption, the volume traded on said candlestick must be taken into account. In order to add confidence to the reading we want to see the volume be relatively high.

Unlike absorption, in the case of the potential initiative we want to see that the closing price is in favor of the imbalance; that is, in the event of a buying initiative we want to see the imbalances at the bottom of the candlestick; and at the top in the event of a selling initiative. This trace suggests to us that there is harmony between that action and the subsequent and immediate movement of the price.

In essence, this candlestick that denotes initiative is the same as the SOS/SOWbar that we work under the Wyckoff methodology, and should therefore comply with its common characteristics:

- Relatively high volume.

- Wide range.

- Close at the end.

Sometimes such a market reversal pattern can be seen in one or two candlesticks (V-turn). Other times, after visualizing a possible absorption, the market will need a greater time consumption before the appearance of the initiative. In the event that the market needs to consume that time before the effective turn occurs, what we want to see to add strength to the idea of absorption is a certain lateralization of the price where the inability of the market to continue in the direction it was leading is glimpsed, it is a very evident sample at times of the action of absorption.

Another interesting detail that would add strength to the reversal pattern is if the market leaves an auction over at the end. This would signal to us the refusal of the traders to continue trading in that direction and this lack of interest would facilitate the turn in the opposite direction. If we are not able to identify the finished auction by analyzing the footprint, we can use the Volume Profile as we have already seen.

Bearish Reversal Pattern: Buying Absorption and Initiative Selling

If at the present moment we are waiting for the development of a bearish trigger, we are going to look to the left of the chart in order to identify any trace that suggests possible absorption of aggressive buying.

As we have already seen with cross-orders, aggressive buys intersect with limited sells and this interaction shows up in the ASK column. Therefore, what we want to see as a sign of possible buying absorption are big deals in the ASK column on or near the trading zone.

But any location of these large negotiations would not be worth it either, the ideal would be to see them on the top of the candlesticks since in case really large traders want to enter with limited selling, they will be at a high price level (they buy cheap and sell expensive).

This possible absorption alone is not enough to enter the market. We need to see aggressiveness that suggests selling intent, and we identify this with the appearance of great negotiations in the BID column. This imprint of the BID is objectively the execution of aggressive sell orders (Sell Market) and given the context in which we find ourselves, we could interpret that the origin and intention of said orders is to enter the market directionally adding selling pressure.

The ideal location where we want these big deals to show up is at the top of the footprint. If, in addition to this, we see a subsequent downward movement of the price, we would be facing another trace that would suggest the aggressive entry of sellers, visually and by methodology, it would appear on the chart as a Sign of Weakness bar (SOWbar).

In this example we see how this pattern of potential buying absorption plus selling initiative appears during the development of two contiguous candlesticks. It would be the exact theoretical representation of what we are looking for: an approach to the trading zone with a movement that denotes a lack of interest, a quasi climatic action where the imbalances in the ASK occur on the top of the candlestick, followed by a candlestick with imbalance in the BID also in its upper part that achieves a certain downward movement and closes at the low of the candlestick (SOWbar).

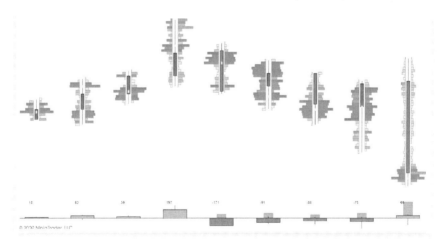

We also see a significant rotation in the Delta going from +197 to -171, suggesting a change of control in favor of the sellers, confirmed by the subsequent bearish reaction.

Bullish Reversal Pattern: Selling Absorption and Initiative Buying

In a context of waiting for the development of the bullish trigger, we will be looking in the first instance for traces that suggest selling absorption. Contrary to what was explained above, this absorption should be shown as strong activity in the BID column. Absorption is a simple block where in this case the price is not dropped. All sell orders that attack the BID are matched with buy limit orders making it impossible to move the price down. It is a very important trace of professional accumulation.

Regarding the location of these major negotiations, we want to see them in the lower part of the footprint as a true reflection of the blockade. If we see those huge volumes at the top, it would make little sense to think about possible selling absorption.

Later, what we want to see is a buying initiative: aggression to the ASK that suggests the intention to enter the market directionally by raising the price. We want to see these imbalances that remain below the closing price of the candlestick, which will suggest that this aggression has had some upward continuity.

In essence, an SOSbar is exactly that, aggression by large traders who achieve a large price movement. The difference is that through candlestick analysis we see the final representation and not the matching orders that occurs within it.

Here we see a genuine theoretical chart of a bullish turn. If we look closely, before the turn, we can already see a potential absorption on the candlestick that marks a -536 Delta. It is a very good example to highlight the importance of the Delta. After that -536 is followed by a bullish candlestick, this is a first indication that we may be facing an absorption since if what was executed there were really aggressive selling, the most logical thing is that it would have continued to fall. Instead the price reacts by going up; but this bullish candlestick does not have much commitment behind it since on the one hand it does not leave any imbalance to support its movement, and on the other hand the delta is not very significant in relation to what was previously seen. Most likely the market is not yet ready to go higher.

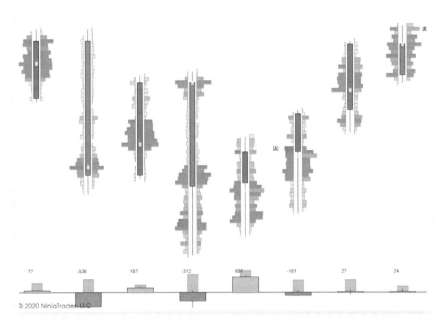

And that is when it develops the effective turn in a two candlestick pattern. New absorptions can be seen in that great first bearish candlestick which is accompanied by a delta of -312 to later appear a candlestick of bullish initiative with imbalances in the ASK, a relatively high volume and a delta of +607, now evidencing a clear rotation in favor of buyers.

CONTINUATION PATTERN

Continuity patterns serve us mainly to confirm the directionality originated in the previous turn as well as allowing us to identify points where to look for incorporation when a trend movement is underway.

This pattern is made up of two actions: the creation of the control and its subsequent test.

Control

This pattern is the clearest sign of interest in one direction. It is displayed on the footprint through imbalances. In essence it is the same as the initiative with the only difference that it occurs once the movement has started.

Although we could determine a control with a single imbalance, it is best to wait for the appearance of at least two. The logic is that the more imbalances traders are able to generate, the stronger that area will be. Again, it must be taken into account that depending on the requirement when parameterizing the software, it will show more or less imbalances. For this reason, we must not confine ourselves to theoretical definitions that are not totally objective. The fact that a single imbalance occurs instead of two or three together does not mean that this event cannot be treated as a control.

This is so because the control action is not only about imbalances; Other characteristics must be met, such as the range of the candlestick, its closing level and the traded volume.

We therefore identify a bullish control when we see imbalances in the ASK column on a candlestick with good volume that manages to close in the upper third of the total range. Preferably, the further down the range of the candlestick the imbalances are, the stronger the stock.

Similarly, we identify a bearish check on imbalances (the higher the range of the candlestick, the better) in the BID column on a high volume bearish candlestick that closes in the lower third of its range. If we have not been able to enter the turn pattern after seeing the absorption plus initiative, the creation of the controls will offer us a new possibility to join as long as there is still a considerable distance with respect to the level where we will establish the objective.

The participants generating the pattern have had the ability to grossly outnumber the contracts traded aggressively over the traders in the opposite column. This action is very relevant since it is not a simple and isolated imbalance, but they have enough momentum to create three imbalances in a row at different price levels.

If after seeing a turn pattern we observe such an appearance on the track it will offer us greater confidence that we are located in favor of the majority of the professional money.

Control test

It is a movement that is going to test a previous area where aggressive traders (controls) have potentially entered. The controls naturally identify a strong zone where the traders that caused the previous imbalance are expected to resurface again should the market revisit the zone.

That is the underlying logic behind that particular action. We are going to favor the fact that these traders are going to defend their position by not letting the price move against them, thus offering us a good opportunity. So what we are going to look for is the development of a new gyre pattern over the area. Zone that will encompass the price levels identified in the control. In this context, the absorption action may not be so noteworthy since the great effort was already made previously. What should be evident is a new show of initiative that suggests the aggressive entry of such traders defending their position. This should be the definitive signal to enter the market.

On some occasions this test will develop very quickly on the next developing candlestick. This will probably be seen as a wick denoting a lack of interest in trading in that area, subsequently leaving a full reversal of the candlestick. At other times there will be a small extension in that area where the price will temporarily appear to breakout through but eventually reverse leaving a rejection. And there will be some occasion when the test leaves it practically at the tick. The key here is to be open-minded and flexible about the representation of said test.

It should be noted that the lack of interest should be evident in this behavior as in any other test action already known under the price and volume analysis. A clear sign of this inactivity, as we already know, would be observable through a relatively low volume.

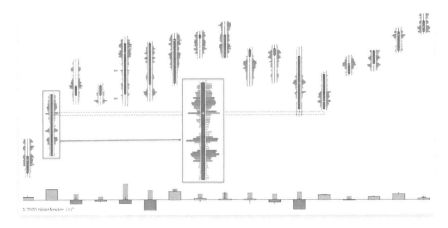

In this example the price comes from generating a bullish turn and is in the middle of the movement. The bullish control is created on that wide range, good volume, positive delta bullish candlestick. We identify the level of the imbalance that also coincides with the VPOC of the candlestick and we extend it to the right as a potential trading area to search for longs. The price subsequently retraces above said level and generates a reversal in two candlesticks with good rotation in the delta. It is interesting to observe how the bearish candlestick reaches this level with a decrease in volume denoting rejection and how later the bullish candlestick generates a large volume leaving a new imbalance in the ASK. From there the price continues its upward development.

In this other example we see how bearish control is generated on a candlestick with large displacement and high volume with a large negative delta suggesting a strong aggressive entry of sellers.

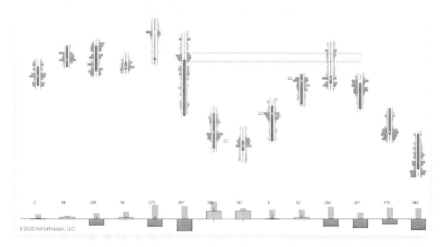

If we look closely, the imbalance in the BID is generated along with other levels that have been highly traded, so we can assume that area as a High Volume Node; and it will be this one that we will project in the future to look for the bearish continuation on it.

In this case, the chart is 15 minutes, so if we want to fine-tune the entry, we could lower the timing to 5 minutes to look for the bearish turn pattern on it: buying absorption and selling initiative. In case we want to continue maintaining the time frame, we would wait for the close of the candlestick that tests said control to evaluate if sellers have entered again and our entry trigger is activated.

The key, as already mentioned above, before two or more imbalances are generated together to treat said action as the control is that even if it is only one, it appears on a candlestick with a wide range, closes near the extreme and a volume relatively high since these are the signs that suggest the entry of large traders.

For the continuation pattern, we could also treat as the control to look for the test that initial imbalance that we identified in the initiative of the turn pattern. Most likely, it meets all the characteristics we are looking for, so it would be the first area to project in which to look for incorporation.

FRACTALITY

Although basically the reading of this type of patterns is oriented to the intraday, this logic can be extrapolated in the same way to higher time frames.

In the pattern of rotation observable in the trace of Order Flow, the absorption and initiative is nothing more than a representation on a tiny scale of what in another temporality would be a cumulative or distributive scheme. We could observe the same pattern of rotation from a slightly larger perspective (during the development of one or several sessions) and it would be visualized in the form of P and b, where the bell is nothing more than a process of absorption inside it, being later represented the initiative as the movement of breakout of the zone of value.

Assuming it on an even larger scale, we would have the medium and long-term structures made up from several days to weeks. These structures represent exactly the same behavior again, where the absorption process would be the accumulation/distribution range, and the initiative would be the trend movement, although on a larger scale.

The only difference is the time consumption that the market needs to complete such an absorption process. In the following example we see how the chart on the left develops it into a three candlestick pattern; in the central one it does it during the development of a session; and in the chart on the right you need to consume several days to carry out the process leaving a clearer structure.

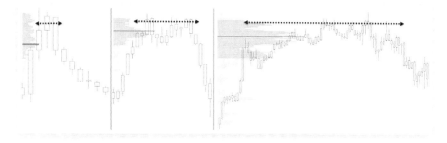

The same goes for continuation patterns. In essence, a control will be part of an impulsive movement while a test of said control will be part of a corrective movement. It is the natural dynamic of trend movements: pushes and pullbacks.

Observing it on a higher scale, we can identify this control in the VPOC if we launch a profile on the entire impulsive section. This VPOC would represent the zone of control for the entire movement. That is why these are levels to take into account on which to look for the end of a possible setback and the start of a new impulse.

And on a longer-term scale, where we try to analyze the general context, we assign the control function over high-volume nodes (HVN), which represent accumulation/distribution structures over other time frames.

In the following chart we see an example of this concept of fractality with controls. We launch a profile of the last impulse and identify the VPOC of said section. This VPOC can be considered as the seller's zone of control, so a good strategy would be to try to incorporate ourselves short in a future test of the zone. The key to understanding the concept is to be clear that if that downward momentum were part of a single candlestick, the most traded level within it would be that VPOC. We also see how said control is generated by a minor redistribution scheme which causes the creation of the High Volume Node.

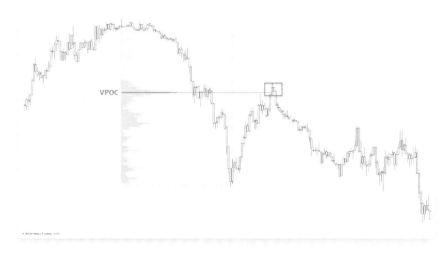

This is the best possible explanation of the fractality of the market. As we can see, the behaviors are always the same regardless of the temporary variable. Here lies one of the advantages of this work methodology. Once this is internalized, we can be in a position to cover with greater solidity the trading in different temporalities.

Free gift #4: Video: Rotation patterns.

To complement the content in this part, I'm giving you a video where I explain how to use the Volume Profile to identify price rotation patterns.

You can access from this link: https://tradingwyckoff.com/book-2/

or by scanning this QR code directly::

PART 5. WYCKOFF 2.0

W̲e come to the final part after presenting what in my view are the strongest principles for discretionary and technical trading in the financial markets.

It is what I have called Wyckoff 2.0

It is about combining the main ideas of the Wyckoff methodology; the principles of auction theory and help us with the Volume Profile and Order Flow tools in order to propose the most robust possible scenarios.

1. Wyckoff Method

It is the cornerstone on which the trading approach is based mainly because it is based on a real underlying logic, because it provides us with a context with which to formulate scenarios and because it offers us different analytical tools with which to be able to evaluate who can have control of the market.

On the one hand, we speak of **underlying logic** due to the theoretical framework behind it. There are many concepts that Richard Wyckoff tried to spread but without a doubt the ones that have achieved the most relevance have been the three fundamental laws and the processes of accumulation and distribution.

Among the three laws, if there is one that stands out as a standard associated with the Wyckoff methodology, it is the Law of Supply and Demand. It is the real engine of the financial markets even though they have evolved. Regardless of the type of participant, intention, valuation or anything that has to do with the positioning of an order, in the end it is about executing a transaction, buying and selling; and this is universal.

In addition, the processes of accumulation and distribution, going hand in hand with the law of cause and effect, offer us a very genuine image of how the market moves. There is no doubt that to visualize an effect in the form of an uptrend it will first be necessary to develop a cumulative cause; and that for a bearish effect to take place, a distributive process will first be necessary. It is quite another matter how such processes will unfold.

On the other hand, the importance of having a clear **context** to guide oneself must be highlighted. This is one of the most important sections of the strategy since it allows us the possibility of proposing certain movements based on how the price is behaving up to the present moment.

We understand that the interaction between supply, demand, buyers and sellers create structures that, although not in form but in substance, are constantly repeated. The genuine identification of these structures helps us to recognize the context in which we find ourselves and from there favor development towards one side or the other. At this point, it is important to highlight what we understand by fractality and how minor structures fit within larger ones.

Finally, the Wyckoff methodology approach provides us with a series of **analytical tools** with which to assess who is gaining control of the market during the development of the structures.

Most of the market actions offer us information about the commitment that buyers and sellers have to gain control. The fact of developing a movement in a specific way or the simple fact of not being able to develop a certain movement leave us very subtle clues with which to evaluate the underlying strength or weakness.

Finally, the analyzes under the Law of Effort and Result are very useful in order to determine the harmony or divergence in the movements. In the end, it is about making the most objective analyzes possible and adding traces in favor of one side or the other until determining who is most likely to be in control.

2. Auction theory

Although Richard Wyckoff did not use these concepts in his studies, **balance and imbalance** are still the reasoning behind lateral and trend movements.

An accumulation and distribution range, terms that Wyckoff did use, are exactly balance zones where buyers and sellers exchange their contracts as a sign of market efficiency, a term used by auction theory. The same happens with the upward and downward trend movements, which essentially represent inefficiency and imbalance.

At the end of the day the underlying logic of the principles of the Wyckoff methodology is based on exactly this, on the theory of the auction, the **acceptance and rejection** of certain areas; and this is what I try to convey to anyone who refers to this approach as an outdated and completely inoperative method for today's markets.

In addition, we incorporate the principle that the market, in order to **facilitate trading** among its participants, will always seek to go to old areas of high activity where both buyers and sellers exchanged a large number of contracts. This principle is tremendously useful for more precise analysis and locating logical areas for taking profits.

3. Volume Profile

The Volume Profile is a tool that objectively **identifies the most important trading zones and levels** based on volume.

For Wyckoff traders, the analysis of the profiles helps us to improve the **identification of structures**, mainly for those cases in which they develop more erratically where the events are not so easily identifiable.

It also allows us to determine the **market bias** through the analysis of trading zones and trading levels; as well as analyze the **health of the trend** through the continuous evaluation of the evolution of value areas.

For those traders who do not take into account the Wyckoff methodology approach, volume profiles also provide context for setting scenarios based on **value area trading principles**. Although it is true that taking into account all the analytical tools offered by the Wyckoff methodology can help us when it comes to favoring trading towards one side or the other, these trading principles by Volume Profile also serve as a road map with which to expect movements. price specifics.

Finally, it can also be tremendously useful to take it into account to calibrate position management; everything to do with trade entry, stop loss placement and take profit setting.

4. Order Flow

After studying in depth everything that has to do with the matching orders and evidencing the problems that its analysis has in an isolated way, we are in a position to limit its use only to the key trading areas.

Due to the discretion involved, using any type of order flow analysis without taking anything else into account doesn't seem like the most robust way to approach it. If in itself it is a subjective tool, not having a clear route map can make the trading become a coin toss.

That's where the importance of having a clear context and an established directional bias comes in again. Only when we are in a potential entry situation is it time, if anything, to put the magnifying glass and observe how the matching orders is taking place to validate our entry trigger.

Having **imbalances** as a fundamental basis, the analysis of the Footprint that is proposed would mainly go through the identification, just at the moment of searching for the trigger, of the two key behaviors in the turns of the market: **absorption** and **initiative**.

In addition, and in case we have not been able to enter such a turn, we still have the possibility to raise an entry with a continuation pattern by identifying **controls plus test**.

Trading plan

Having as a fundamental basis the perception of value that we have studied with the auction theory, the context and the analytical tools that the Wyckoff methodology offers us, as well as the analysis of levels and trading zones that we identify by Volume Profile, we are going to propose different trading strategies.

In order to facilitate the understanding of this section, a diagram is presented as a summary of the entire process:

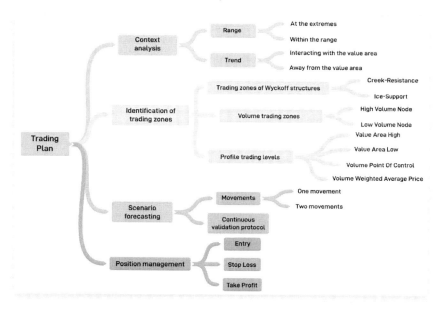

ANALYSIS OF THE CONTEXT

The first thing we must do when analyzing any chart is to identify the context in which the price is found: range or trend. The main function is to bias ourselves directionally by applying an trading according to its condition and determine what we want to do, whether to buy or sell.

Let's see a brief summary of the trading possibilities depending on the context:

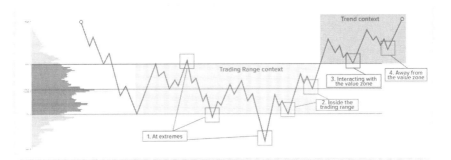

In this chart we have an ideal scheme of accumulation. We see how the trading context offered by the Wyckoff methodology converges with the trading principles by Volume Profile. Within the top three extreme trading opportunities (1) of the range context would fit with the principle of range trading by Volume Profile.

After the Spring, the price recovers the value area and we see again the confluence of both principles: by Wyckoff methodology we would look for a test at the top of the structure while by Volume Profile the reversal trading would be activated where we would look for the visit to the extreme opposite of the value area of the profile. This movement to the opposite extreme would be in a position to take advantage of it firstly on the Spring and secondly if it leaves us with an trading opportunity inside (2), either on the potential test of the Spring or on some superior LPS.

Once the price leaves the balance range, we would be in a trend context and in this situation, the first trading opportunity would be in the test after breakout (3) where, by Wyckoff methodology, we would look for the incorporation on the Creek; and based on the trading principles by Volume Profile, the continuation trading scenario would be activated, in which case we would do it on the extreme of the value area, in this bullish example on the Value Area High.

When the price is already in the middle of the trend movement, we would have to work with the context away from the value area (4) where we would expect some kind of setback to seek incorporation into the current movement.

Range Context

It is about the construction of the cause of the subsequent trend movement which will be up or down.

This rotation phase can appear during the course of one or several sessions (even weeks). If it contains several sessions, it is best to draw a volume profile together in order to identify the trading areas globally.

• **At extremes of the range**. If we observe the stop of the previous trend movement and a certain later lateralization, we will determine that we are in a range context within an balance zone and the trading here would be based on the search for reversals at the extremes of the structure; that is, buy below and sell above.

• **Inside the range**. If we are inside a large range and we have enough space, we can also set up an trading looking for the extremes. Especially recommended when we have seen a false breakout previously that provides us with a clearer directional context.

Trend Context

When a trend is identified, the trader should only trade with it, waiting for retracements to try and enter the market.

  • **In trend interacting with the value area**. If after sideways an inefficiency occurs that throws the price out of an balance zone, we must evaluate the possibility that it is an effective breakout or a false breakout. If the traces analyzed previously suggest that it could be the actual breakout, the trading here will be based on the search for the confirmation test on the broken structure or at some more immediate trading level.

  • **In the trend away from the value area**. Once the effective breakout of the previous balance zone has been confirmed, the price will now be in a trend context and the acceptance of these new levels where it is trading makes us base the trading in favor of that direction.

The question that we must constantly be asking ourselves is what context the market is currently in. Your answer will determine the type of strategy to apply. As we already know, the only two conditions in which the market can be in are in balance or in Imbalance. So basically we are going to be working in range and trend trading.

Next we will delve into each of the trading contexts:

Range Trading

Mainly we are going to distinguish two scenarios within range trading depending on the price in relation to the analyzed balance zone:

At the extremes

That the price is trading within a value area suggests that the balance is total between buyers and sellers. Neither of them has control and therefore the price is expected to continue moving in the same dynamics.

The trading context here would be to favor reversals at the extremes:

• By Wyckoff methodology, it would be a matter of looking for the entry **into the false breakout in Phase C**. In other words, if we are facing the upper part of the structure, we will favor the Upthrust; while if we are in the lower part we will look for the Spring. Its genuine development will suggest a visit to the opposite end of the structure.

• By Volume Profile it would be a question of trading the reversal **on the limits of the value area**. We would therefore look for the bearish turn on the Value Area High and the bullish turn on the Value Area Low. A rejection of such areas would suggest visiting the opposite end of the value area.

Inside

On the other hand, if the range is wide enough, some scenario could be considered within it. By Wyckoff methodology, in case of observing that the price has possibly developed the test event in Phase C, it would be the **entry into the trend movement within the range in Phase D**. The only necessary filter would be that it had enough travel available to offer a good risk/reward ratio.

In that case, we would need to be positioned in favor of as many trading levels as possible. The fact that the price is able to reach one of those levels and breakout it effectively will suggest to us that there is some control on the part of the traders in that direction. If we are also in favor of a High Volume Node, we would already have identified the market bias.

Within a wide profile we can identify different areas of high and low trading. We must remember that the last High Volume Node generated will be the one that determines the directional bias at least in the shortest term. As long as the price remains above, we will only propose bullish scenarios and vice versa if it is below.

• A High Volume Node is a lateralization of the price. By pure logic, if we are above it, we can suggest that this HVN is an accumulation. Therefore, to buy we want to be protected with an accumulation below.

• Conversely with distributions. If we are below a HVN it will be identified as a distribution, which makes us think that favoring shorts would be the most appropriate.

This type of trading within the range will be subject to necessarily managing the position when reaching the extremes of the balance zone, since in principle we must continue to favor that neither side has total control until the final imbalance is caused. .

Supported by the trading principles of Volume Profile, in the event that the price comes from making a false breakout, we would be in a reversal trading context applying the adapted rule of 80% where the probability, after re-entering the value area, is in the visit from the opposite end.

Trend Trading

After a movement of intentionality that breaks the balance and in which the traces analyzed suggest that the imbalance is on one side or the other, we are going to seek to trade in favor of that direction, waiting for a test at some relevant trading level.

Interacting with the value area

New information has entered the market causing the imbalance and the first thing to evaluate is that it is not a failed breakout that generates a false breakout with re-entry back into the value area.

If the traces suggest that this is an effective breakout our bias now should be to look for some trade idea in favor of that direction.

- Under the Wyckoff methodology, if we observe an impulsive movement that intentionally breaks the structure, we would seek **entry into the Phase D breakout test**.

- This type of trading is also useful for traders who do not trade structures. The logic is exactly the same. Based on pure Volume Profile analysis, we could wait for the price to leave a certain value area and wait for it to enter the test, it would be the continuation trading under the Volume Profile trading principles.

To try to determine if we are indeed facing a potential genuine breakout, we are going to analyze different traces. This is the moment to go back over the content in the section "How to distinguish between accumulation and distribution?".

As main traces to try to clarify if the breakout will be genuine we will take into account:

1. **The false breakout**. Key action, the search for liquidity The deeper the false breakout, the stronger the stage. Although there are occasional local shocks (above some high or low within the range), we will initially wait for the full false breakout as it gives us more confidence.

2. **Price action and volume after the shakeout and at the breakout**. Candles with good movement and high volume denoting control by one of the sides (buyers or sellers). At the moment of the breakout, since we are facing a liquidity zone, it is likely that a relatively high volume will appear and even a wick will be visually observed. This is normal and should not initially lead us to think that it could be a false breakout since the behavior of the absorption has this characteristic: high volume and possibility of wicking. The key is what happens next.

3. **The reaction after the breakout looking for the non-re-entry to the range**. After the breakout of a value area we must wait for the price to gain acceptance at those new levels where it will be trading. This will be evidenced initially with a sideways market out of the range.

   A sample that would add greater strength to the acceptance scenario would be to observe the migration of the VPOC to that new area or the creation of a new one (perhaps that of a later session). This initially represents acceptance, but we would still have to wait to confirm the action, as we saw in the section on VPOC migration.

   And the definitive trace is obtained by visualizing the non-re-entry back to the value area, to the range. At that point we will already have a change in the perception of value: price + time + volume where the probability would be in the continuation in favor of the breakout movement.

   To point out that the consumption of time after the breakout should not be excessive. Enough to generate a new VPOC or its migration, but the moment this happens, the price should start the trend movement. The momentum behind the first imbalance should cause continuity with some speed.

Once the price manages to position itself and stay outside the value area, we will determine that an imbalance has occurred, that said movement has not been rejected, and therefore we will be in a position to seek incorporation in favor of that direction.

• If we are in a potential bullish breakout, all the volume seen below, as well as that previous zone of balance, can now be identified as a potential accumulation. As we know, the effect of an accumulation will be a trending move higher and this is where we want to be positioned.

• Conversely, when we find ourselves in a situation of possible bearish breakout, if the price is capable of holding said zone and not re-entering the previous balance area, we will be in a position to identify such a process as distributive and it will be time to look for the trigger with which enter the sell to take advantage of the subsequent bearish trend movement.

Away from the value area

We may start looking at a chart where the price is already outside a certain value area and is moving in search of a new balance area. In this context of trend movement, it is best to wait for the development of a test on any of the trading levels that we identify.

At this point it is convenient to remember the teachings of Richard Wyckoff about how the markets move. It is known by all that they do so in the format of bullish and bearish waves: therefore, the proposed scenario necessarily involves waiting for that wave that will have a corrective nature before continuing in the direction of the trend imbalance.

The key now would be to identify possible areas on which to expect the price to develop said corrective movement. By Wyckoff methodology, it would be about looking for the **entry in the trend movement outside the range in Phase E**. It is a confusing context since this trading according to methodology goes through the search for new intentionality candlesticks (SOS/SOWbar), minor structures and new shakeouts (Ordinary Shakeout/Upthrust), but it does not suggest the location on which to expect the development of these behaviors.

Here we see the importance of working with these levels and trading zones based on volume. They help us determine clearer locations where the price is likely to go as well as give us one more footprint to analyze the health of the trend. The ideal scenario, for example, would be to wait for the development of a minor structure over the area where an trading level such as the weekly VWAP or any other is located.

A very interesting concept is that we will continue to trade in favor of the latest accumulation/distribution until the market develops a structure in the opposite direction or until it loses the last identified value area.

In a trend context we are going to point out the last area of relevant high volume that is supporting said movement. That is, if we are in an uptrend we will have the last high trading node (HVN) below the current price very present and if we are in a downtrend we will have identified the last HVN just above the price. These nodes will be the ones that will ultimately determine the change of control of the market. Therefore, we will only propose a scenario against the trend when said zone is crossed. To delve into this concept, review again the determination of the market bias through the analysis of the trading zones seen in the section on the uses of Volume Profile.

IDENTIFYING TRADING ZONES AND LEVELS

Once we know the context and have determined what we want to do (buy or sell), the second has to do with where. It is about identifying the exact location on which we will expect the price to develop our entry trigger. The zones and levels will vary depending on the type of strategy to apply.

The trading logic is exactly the same for all contexts, profiles and timeframes: identify the trading areas and levels and wait for our trigger to confirm the imbalance and enter the market.

Depending on the type of trading you do, you can adapt these same concepts to your operations.

- If you are a **day trader** you may use the profile of the previous session as a basis for setting up scenarios and the profile of the current session as support.

- If you are a **longer-term trader**, you may find it more interesting to analyze the profile of the previous week as a basis to identify the trading zones; o a Composite profile to cover weeks or months and to be able to identify the zones of high and low negotiation; as well as taking into account the VWAP of higher temporalities such as weekly and monthly.

- If you are a **structures trader**, it may be best to pull fixed profiles anchored to the work structures and propose scenarios based on their trading areas.

Or maybe what works best for you is to do a mix of all of the above. In the end, each trader must do an individual job to determine which way they feel most comfortable, since there is no universal rule about which profile to work with. What is important is that the concepts are just as valid for different trading contexts.

For this point, it is useful to be clear that the profiles that have already been completed have greater relevance than the profiles in progress. By pure logic, a profile that is still in development is susceptible to modification in its levels and therefore the importance that we can grant to them decreases. On the other hand, the profiles that have already been finalized ultimately represent the final consensus of the market and their levels acquire greater relevance.

There is no general rule regarding how much time period Composite profiles should cover. You may want to take into account the last week, the current week, the last month, the current month or the current year. Here you necessarily have to decide discretionally. There is no better profile than another and that is why it is the trader's job to determine which one to work with. What is recommended is that these profiles cover enough price action both above and below the current price in order to be able to identify the key trading areas, mainly high and low volume nodes.

The search for the trigger to enter will therefore be done exclusively on the areas already indicated, distinguishing between:

- Trading areas of structures under the Wyckoff methodology.

- Volume trading zones: HVN and LVN.

- Profile trading levels: VAH, VAL, VPOC and VWAP.

Depending on the trading context, we will favor waiting over one level or another:

At extremes of the range

It is the classic Wyckoff trading in the zone of potential false breakout of the maximum/minimum of the structure. The false breakout itself can be operated as a more aggressive entry and the false breakout test as a more conservative entry.

- **VAH/VAL**. Taking into account the trading levels of the Volume Profile, we will also be in a position to look for the reversal on the extremes of the value area, which will sometimes coincide with the extremes of the structure. Range trading.

Inside the range

Always keeping in mind that we will have to find ourselves in favor of a High Volume Node and with enough travel we will wait for the price on:

- **LVN**. Low volume nodes by their very nature establish excellent areas on which to look for potential opportunities. In this context, the ideal will be to identify these areas through a profile that covers the entire range.

- **VWAP and VPOC**. Either that of the current session for more intraday traders or that of a profile that covers several of them for structure traders.

These are the levels that determine the control of the market, so we will wait for the price to produce the effective breakout on them and we will look for the first entry to the test of them.

Said test could only be given on the closest level, although it is true that the confluence of both adds greater strength to the scenario.

Sometimes the price after producing this breakout will not leave any test and the momentum will make the price move quickly, so a more aggressive entry would occur after the intentional movement that breaks these levels occurs.

In trend interacting with the value area

After the beginning of the imbalance and having already evaluated the possibility of continuity of the movement, we are going to wait for a setback to assess the entry on:

- **Level of the broken structure**. For the structure trader it is another of the classic Wyckoff entries: Entry in the breakout and retest. Initially we will wait for the price in the broken Creek/Ice area, which by its very nature will be a Low Volume Node. Out of the corner of our eye, we will also be aware of the nearby trading levels so as not to rule out entry in case the price goes looking for any of these, mainly the end of the value area.

- **Extremes of the value area**. The intraday trader or simply does not trade taking into account structures could value the entry after leaving a certain value area (for example that of the current session) and wait for the price to make a test at the extremes of its Value Area to enter. Continuation trading

- **Range VPOC**. It will be the last trading level on which to expect the pullback after the breakout. If it is very far from the broken end, it is best to quarantine the scenario since at that point the price will have re-entered the value area and will already have some depth. In this case, and under the trading principles of Volume Profile, the type of failed reversal trading that manages to recover the end of the value area should be activated.

In the trend away from the value area

Imbalance context so we will already have an HVN (accumulation/distribution) in our favor.

We should expect some pullback at whatever trading level the price is at. If the first level is too close, it is most likely that it will look for the next one to develop a setback with a certain proportionality in relation to the previous impulse.

- **Previous Session Profile Levels**. Generally, and because we are in a trend context, the levels that the price will find before will correspond to those of the previous session (Extremes of the Value Area, VWAP and VPOC). As the day unfolds, we can also propose some scenario about the levels of the current session.

- **Weekly VWAP**. We will always be very aware of the location of the weekly VWAP since it is especially useful in these trend contexts to look for the end of the retracement and the beginning of a new impulsive movement.

- **VPOC of the previous impulse**. In addition, we can draw a fixed profile of the last price impulse and have located the location of its VPOC, since we already know that it is also a very interesting area on which to wait for the price.

- **LVN**. It is interesting to identify the low volume zones within the context that we are trading. In this case we can use different profiles: composite to identify the general context; previous impulse profile and profile of previous sessions.

For all contexts we will want to trade in favor of as many trading levels as possible. It is interesting to point out that the confluence zones of trading levels are highly recommended to search for entries, highlighting the combination of VPOC and VWAP.

SCENARIO FORECASTING

Once we have a clear context, that we know the type of strategy that we are going to try to execute and that we have identified the location on which to wait for the entry trigger, it is time to set the stage. This part has to do with how.

Normally the scenario to look for the entry trigger will be composed of one or two movements depending on the current location of the price:

One movement

The price will already be positioned in favor of our idea and therefore we should only expect a simple action that will take the price towards the trading zone.

If based on the context what we want is to buy, we are going to identify the trading levels that we have below where the price is likely to go.

If, on the other hand, once the context analysis has been done, we determine that the most optimal thing is to trade for sell, we will identify the most immediate trading levels above which to look for the short entry trigger.

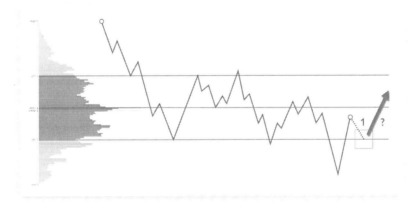

In this example we see that we are in a range context and in a situation of potential Spring, so the scenario approach would be to wait for a single movement that would develop the test and look for the buy entry trigger.

Two movements

We may only want to buy or sell if certain price action occurs.

If, based on the analysis of the context, what we want is to buy, but the price is below the operative zone, we must wait for a first positioning movement above said zone and a second test movement. After that we would be in a position to look for the entry trigger.

The same would happen if what we want is to sell but the price is above the trading zone; in this case we should expect a first recovery movement of the area and a second test movement.

In this other example, the reading we do is that we are in a range context in which the price comes from developing a potential Spring and has serious possibilities that it is a cumulative range.

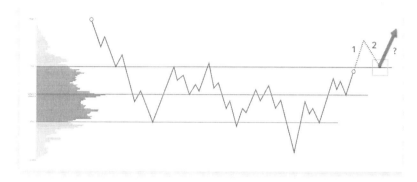

At that precise moment and knowing the route map offered by the methodology, we would be in a position to wait for the buy entry after seeing the upward breakout (1) plus the subsequent test (2). For context we want to buy but the price is not in an operationally attractive area (since it is going to face the key area) so it is appropriate to propose a two-move scenario.

As we know, the price could leave an Upthrust at 1 and re-enter the price back into balance, but initially we should be directionally biased to the upside after seeing the downside false breakout and breakout move meet the expectations. characteristics.

The market obviously will not always follow our approaches. A lot of times we will see how we are forced to change our sentiment based on what the price has been doing. This is the key to the continuous analysis of the reaction of the participants as new information arrives in the market.

The best way to approach this scenario planning process is through a continuous validation protocol. It's about actively reacting to what the market does (If X, then maybe Y). This means that "If the price does this, then we will expect that". It is an optimal approach to know at all times what to expect the price to do and to be prepared to act with the speed that is required.

"If the price breaks the Creek, then I'm going to wait for him to test for buys. If, on the other hand, there is a failed breakout, then I will wait for a test in the opposite direction to enter short"

The key here is to assess all the possible options that the market can develop and, even if we are initially directionally biased to one side, we should always also take into account an alternative scenario in the opposite direction that allows us to make a quick bias change in case necessary.

We have an example when the market faces the top of a structure. We are in the trading zone, in a situation of potential bullish breakout or false breakout. It may be that by context we are directionally biased to favor the bullish breakout and are therefore looking to buy the breakout test; But when the time comes, what we see is that the price re-enters the range again, strongly refusing to go up and leaving what looks like an upward jolt (Up-thrust). At that point we should have enough capacity to read this in real time and change the stage approach to find the short.

MANAGING THE TRADE

Although it is true that the most important element of this combination is undoubtedly everything that the Wyckoff methodology offers us, we have already seen that the Volume Profile and Order Flow tools can be certainly useful when it comes to improving our planning approaches. scenarios and operations.

Thanks to the principles of the Wyckoff methodology we will be in a position to propose scenarios; thanks to the identification of the trading zones and levels by Volume Profile we will be able to fine-tune where the price is most likely to go; and thanks to the precision of the Order Flow it will allow us to further confirm and calibrate the input trigger.

Entry

Regardless of the trading context, the market entry trigger will always be an action that denotes intentionality on the part of the large trader in favor of our direction.

For pure price action analysis we will continue working with intentionality candlesticks: SOSbar (Sign of Strength Bar) and SOWbar (Sign of Weakness Bar):

- Sign of Strength Bar (SOSbar). Clear conviction on the part of the buyers. This is generally represented by a bullish candlestick, with a wide body and range, a closing price in the upper third and moderately high volume.

- Sign of Weakness Bar (SOWbar). Aggressive sellers. Depicted by a bearish candlestick, with a wide body and range, a closing price in the lower third and moderately high volume.

These candlesticks represent a movement in one direction or the other. Buyers or sellers have gained control by trading more aggressively than the other side.

For the trader who wants to observe the Order Flow, I would only recommend working with the concepts already explained:

- Turn pattern: absorptions and initiatives.

- Continuation pattern: controls and test.

In essence, what we would look for in the turn pattern would be to confirm that the SOS/SOWbar is leading; and in case of losing the initial trigger we could look for a re-entry in the continuation pattern.

Entry order

As we saw in the section on the types of orders, participants can enter the market in different ways, basically with Market, Stop or Limit orders.

In our case we are going to use Stop orders. We remember that these are located above the current price if what we want is to buy; and below the current price if what we want is to sell.

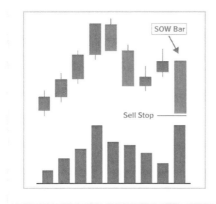 

With the development of the intention candlestick we have an obvious sign of interest, but it is interesting to use the Stop orders as a definitive filter that suggests a certain continuity in the movement started with the trigger candlestick.

Sometimes we will see the development of what initially looks like an intention candlestick and right after it closes the price reverses sharply in the opposite direction. What has happened is that an absorption process has been carried out internally at all those price levels and traders with greater capacity were positioning themselves on the opposite side. By using this type of order, although it is true that we are not saved from this potential situation, on many occasions where this is happening it will prevent us from entering the market.

If we really are facing a movement of imbalance, it will have a strong momentum where pressure will continue in favor of that direction. With this type of limit order we will be entering in favor of momentum, of imbalance.

In any case, this section should be evaluated more in depth by the trader. You may prefer to enter a market order after the trigger candlestick closes, after seeing an aggression in the footprint without waiting for the candlestick to close, or even use a limit order to enter a possible pullback. Any option could be valid.

Why You Shouldn't Enter Limit Orders

Simply because you would be betting that the movement you expect will take place, and if you remember, we are managing an environment of total uncertainty so we do not know what is going to happen.

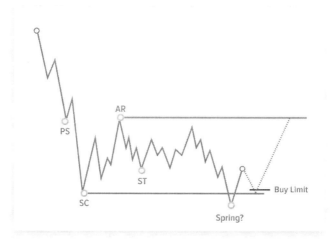

For example, you may see a chart in a potential Spring situation. If the analysis is correct, we know that the route map offered by the methodology goes through the search for at least the upper part of the structure; so you may think that it is a good option to place a Buy Limit entry order waiting for the Spring test to develop.

But it is possible that said test will never take place and instead the price will continue to fall confirming that our analysis was not correct, which would make us add a loss. The problem is not assuming that loss, since it is part of the business, but rather that the basic approach was not the most solid.

At the point where you see the potential Spring and place the Buy Limit you are betting that the price will develop two movements: the bearish one to generate the test and the bullish one that will take the price to the high part of the range. And the key is that we can only propose the development of a movement.

In this case, we could initially consider the bearish test movement since we are in a position of potential Spring; and once the price reaches the area where it "should" turn, we have to analyze again the price action and the volume to see if there is that imbalance that generates the bullish turn and then we can consider the next move higher down to the creek.

The basic idea is that we must make a continuous analysis of the interaction between buyers and sellers; and although we are directionally biased to one side based on the context, we must confirm when the time comes that the approach is sound and that the market itself confirms it.

If in a potential test position of the Spring we see that aggressive buyers appear that push the price up, it is the trace that we would need to see to confirm that our analysis seems correct and in that case it would offer us an trading opportunity. We must also remember that the fact of seeing our entry trigger on the proposed area has nothing to do with the fact that said trading later comes out in profit or loss. As we have already seen, new information is constantly entering the market and this could change the perception of value by participants at any time.

Stop Loss

From a pure Wyckoff methodology point of view, we will continue to recommend placing the stop loss on the other side of the intention candlesticks (SOS/SOW bar) and structures. The logic is that if the big traders have been actively involved in these developments they will defend their position in case the price goes against them.

Additionally, we will always want to place the Stop loss on the other side of the more levels and trading zones the better.

The first zone we are going to be looking for will be a Low Volume Node (LVN). As we have already mentioned, due to its very nature, this low trading zone may act in the form of a rejection and that is exactly what we are looking for: that in the event that the price reaches said zone, a V-turn is caused and that said rejection protect our position.

Note that the other way to represent rejection is for price to quickly breakout through these price levels. If so, it would surely reach and execute our protective stop. As we do not know what could happen, we must necessarily use this type of zone with the initial premise that the type of rejection it represents in a possible future visit is that of the V-turn.

The logic of using the rest of the trading levels to protect the position basically lies in the fact that a high amount of volume will be traded on them and could also act as levers that cause a price reversal. Some might think that if these levels act like magnets due to the liquidity that is located on them, why use them to protect the position? If we are bought and we have them at the bottom, based on the principle that they act like magnets, wouldn't it be logical to think that the price will go looking for them? The logic here is that at the time of entry we are working towards a price imbalance seeking its continuation. And therefore it is the moment in which the price will move away from such levels that in general represent balance and acceptance by all. If, at the moment of truth, the imbalance is not such, we still have the possibility of saving the position if participants who turn the market re-enter at those levels.

If we find ourselves in a situation of potential Spring and we see the appearance of an SOSbar, we would be in a position to enter the market with a Buy Stop order at the breakout above the candlestick leaving the Stop Loss location or below the candlestick itself. trigger (#1) or below the entire structure (#2).

At any of these two points, the Stop Loss would be protected firstly by the imbalances generated in the trigger candlestick; by some VWAP that has been generated, and by the Value Area Low of the profile of the structure, which is essentially the Low Volume Node.

In this bearish example, if the SOWbar that offers us the short entry trigger appears, we would place the Sell Stop order below its low and we would also have several Stop Loss locations: just above its high (#1), at the highest maximum generated in the turn (#2) and across the VPOC of the profile (#3).

We would be protected by the sail itself, by some VWAP and by the Low Value Area of the profile which, in addition to being a Low Volume Node, in this case coincides with the ICE (support) of the structure.

A point should be made regarding the VPOC of the profile. In this example we have it a little further away but it is still a relevant level to take into account. The trader should analyze if placing the Stop at that level would still have an acceptable Risk: Reward ratio.

This is one of the peculiarities of discretionary approaches and it is that we must adapt to the behavior of the market. Sometimes all the levels will come together in a very narrow range giving us greater confidence; while others will certainly be separated and we will have to evaluate which location is more optimal and if the risk is worth it.

Take Profit

In my first book "The Wyckoff Methodology in Depth" I already listed the possible actions that we could use to take profits. We mainly talked about:

1. **Climate bar evidence**. Especially useful when we don't have any reference to the left of the chart.

2. **After the development of Phase A** that stops the previous trend, and the potential Phase C of that structure.

3. **In liquidity zones** generated by relevant price movements (previous highs and lows).

Thanks to the incorporation of the Volume Profile we can add a new objective way that is even more useful when we have price negotiations in the direction where we want to take profits.

4. In areas of high prior negotiation

It is about using the High Volume Nodes that we have in the direction of the trading. We already know the magnetic nature of such areas and therefore they give us some confidence to use them as targets.

Supported by auction theory, after an imbalance the market will seek to find traders with the opposite bias who are willing to trade again. That is why the price will move to those areas where there was previously a high negotiation since the same thing is expected to happen again.

It is very important to remember again the short-term mentality of the market where the latest trading areas will have a greater relevance in terms of price attraction than the older areas.

The concept of High Volume Node when setting the goal could be a bit ambiguous. The HVN is a zone, and the order to take profit is a specific price level, where exactly to place it? For this purpose, it is very interesting to take into account the VPOC of that particular value area. The HVN helps us to identify the probable zone of visit of the price and its VPOC for the exact location of the target.

For more intraday trading, it can be extremely useful to have the **Developing Volume Point of Control** (DVPOC) identified. These are price levels that were at a given time the VPOC of a session, regardless of whether or not they were the final VPOC of said session. As we know, the VPOC of the session changes based on the negotiations that take place, and this level represents that trace of change. In short, what it is about is a high negotiation level and therefore, it is most likely that it will have a certain magnetic behavior.

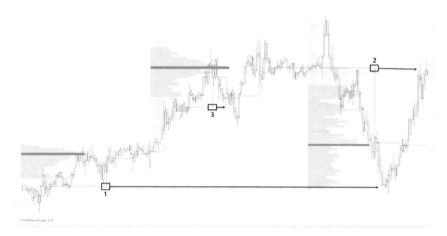

In this example we see how the price distributes in that profile in the form of P and the bearish development goes to look for an old DVPOC below (1) and from there it turns again in the form of V to test again another DVPOC of the current session above (2).

A highlight of the DVPOC that we only take into account those that have not been tested. In this example we see other DVPOCs that have already been tested and therefore would not be valid for the establishment of objectives, as would be case 3.

The same would happen with **naked VPOCs**. We have not discussed this level before because its usefulness is focused almost exclusively as a possible target level. Naked VPOCs are VPOCs from previous sessions that have not been tested. Unlike the DVPOCs, the naked VPOCs were the definitive VPOC of the session. There are statistics that claim that VPOCs from previous sessions are tested on the following days with a high probability. That is why they are very interesting to take into account.

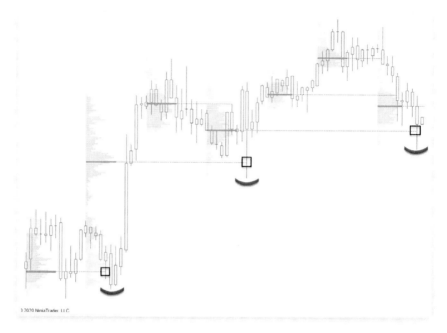

In this other example we see the magnetism exerted by these levels attracting the price and even generating a subsequent turn.

In both graphs, different configurations have been used to specifically visualize one or another level (DVPOC and nakedVPOC). It is recommended to use both as by their very nature both represent previous high trading zones.

Advanced management concepts

In this section we are going to include more complex ideas about market analysis and position management. All concepts explained are based on logic. This is our best tool for understanding all the elements at a high level of detail.

Entry Type "by Context"

In addition to the classic post types, since we are studying advanced content it might already be convenient to explain a more complex post type, I have called it "by context":

This type of entry is based on the idea of prioritizing the development of the structure and the context it offers us over any other element. That is why any decision-making based on this idea should meet the minimum and recommended characteristics that any trading idea based on the analysis of structures should have.

Hand in hand with this new idea, we will take the opportunity to recall the most important elements of the methodology:

Genuine structure

That is, the more closely it resembles the basic schematics, the better. In particular we are going to look at two elements:

• **The Law of Cause and Effect**. That a significant cause has already been built, which will be appreciated with a relatively larger Phase B than any other phase.

• **Overall volume**. Until the onset of the jolt, how the volume has been distributed over the course of the range is a subtle imprint that adds strength to our scenarios. As a general rule we will want to identify:

- A diminishing volume for accumulative structures.

- High volumes or unusual peaks for distribution structures.

The most important market actions

The following three events are the key actions that we should continually be looking for in structure analysis.

Its appearance in a sequential process generates a change of character and identifies the trading event that will determine our directional bias:

• **False breakout**. We are going to wait for it to appear compulsorily since it is the most decisive action in the market.

Remember that we are trying to find the ideal scenario. We could have seen a local false breakout instead of a false breakout to the full extremes, but that behavior is not ideal; the ideal is to have seen a false breakout to the highs and lows of the structure, the bigger and more violent, the better.

• **Breakout**. If the false breakout is genuine, intentionality candlesticks will appear that will take the price to the opposite extreme and beyond, breaking the structure.

We already know the characteristics of the type of candlestick we expect to see here: candlesticks with wide ranges, good distance, closing at their extremes and accompanied by an increase in volume.

• **Test**. The breakout movement can be done with a relatively high or low volume, this footprint is not decisive due to the different interpretations that we can conclude based on the Law of Supply and Demand and how the displacement can occur.

As we studied in my second book "The Wyckoff Methodology in Depth" and specifically in the section on the confirmation event, the key is in:

- That the test movement denotes a lack of interest, that is, with narrow-range, zigzagging up and down candlesticks with low volume, less than in the breakout movement.

- That the price does not re-enter the range. The main signal that indicates that the breakout may be real is that the price stays out of the range and that it fails in its attempts to re-enter the balance zone.

In this way, the combination of the two elements that make up the genuine structure together with the three elements of the operative trinomial offer us the best possible context for our scenario proposals. It is right at that moment that we should be looking for the appearance of our market entry trigger.

And here lies one of the problems that we can find in real operations, what to do if we cannot be in front of the screen at that moment? Perhaps the most logical solution would be to discard the trading and not enter the market since we cannot verify the appearance of our trigger.

And the second option we can take is to prioritize the development of the general context over the appearance of the trigger. That is the rationale for the "by context" input type. If after doing our analysis we determine that we are in the best possible context thanks to the identification of these traces, all this should have more weight than that last action in particular that the trigger represents.

That is why this option is a good alternative, especially if we are analyzing medium and long-term charts. When it comes to managing the position size, we can apply an active management of the pyramiding type already explained in my previous books. If we do not want to enter with the full amount that we had determined, we can divide the entry into two blocks; making a first input now, based on the idea of "input by context", and the rest of the position, for example, after verifying the appearance of our input trigger.

The fact of making the entry without having identified the trigger beforehand can cause us to doubt where to place the Stop Loss. In this case, the most sensible thing would be to place it at some point within the structure where, if it is reached, it presents us with a possibility of false breakout instead of effective breakout. To be specific, the middle of the range could be a good place to locate it.

The Volume of the Structures

As we know, the volume informs us about the participation of the agents. Thanks to the analysis of both the classic vertical volume and the horizontal volume profile, we can identify the level of interest that the structures have generated from their beginning to their completion.

In volume operated in each structure, it is essentially the cause that will have the subsequent trend effect; and that cause, the origin, will greatly influence the general context of the market. In other words, the more volume has been generated in a structure, the more power and influence it will have on future price action.

Underlying this principle is the Law of Cause and Effect: the greater the cause (volume), the greater the effect (price shift).

We can materialize this idea as a tool to improve our reading of the market. We are left with the idea that the higher the volume, the greater the control. What trading use can we give it then? A reasonably simple one and that we study with the Law of Effort and Result, specifically when we try to analyze the price action in the next displacement. We remember:

• If we want to treat a movement as an impulse, we will expect to see that high volume at its origin, which would indicate an institutional presence supporting said movement and that the probability is a continuation in that direction.

• If we see that a movement is generated without a large volume at its origin, objectively it would appear to be a movement without any institutional participation. This suggests to us that this movement is a correction or, in the case of an impulse, it would denote divergence.

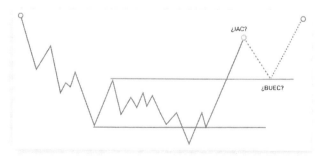

So, we are going to get into a bullish breakout situation after a potential accumulation. Thanks to the context provided by the Wyckoff methodology, if all traces are in line with what we expect to see, our scenario at that point is that a JAC (bullish breakout move) develops to generate the subsequent BUEC (test after move). breakout) with which to confirm the nature of the structure and wait from there for the market to start the upward trend movement outside the range.

We are now going to focus on studying the anatomy of the JAC. As we want to favor the development of a cumulative scheme, our interests would happen because in said action a large amount of volume is not generated to support the subsequent downward movement that will visit the trading level of the broken structure. Based on the aforementioned principle, if we want to treat a movement with a corrective nature instead of an impulsive one, we expect to see it originate without a large volume, denoting a lack of institutional participation in said movement. And this is just what is in line with our approach since we later want a successful Test After Breakout (BUEC) move to develop.

This reading is therefore a significant footprint to take into account when analyzing the behavior of the market after the breakout of the structure with the aim of trying to determine if it is more likely that the breakout is genuine and continues the trend outside the range, or if based on the reaction of the price and the volume it will be more likely that a false breakout (false breakout) will be generated that will re-enter the price back into the range.

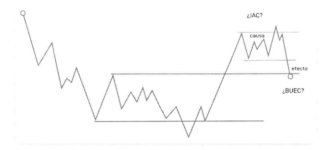

The scenario that a priori offers us the worst perspective regarding the nature of the JAC is therefore that a distribution scheme develops at its origin, which will be the cause of the subsequent downward movement that will test the structure. In this context, we would observe how this bearish movement is being supported by a significant cause that has even managed to generate a complete structure. Structure that would identify the interest of the participants and would represent that there is some bearish control in the context of the market, at least in the short term. The entity of said structure would have to be analyzed in order to draw more objective conclusions.

The idea is that we are left with the fact that if all our previous analysis suggests that we may possibly be facing a potential cumulative structure, that at the moment of the breakout and the subsequent movement that the test is going to develop, we ideally want to see a fast scheme, we want that do not build a cause with a large volume that supports said movement.

The objective of posing this situation is only to learn to identify the common characteristics of the ideal structures, which in the long run will be the ones with the greatest probability of success. Obviously, the fact that this behavior develops does not mean that the potential accumulation is completely discarded. It is simply a sign which should be taken into account. It will be the subsequent market reaction that ultimately tells us what is most likely to happen.

The market could develop a smaller distributive scheme in the JAC but hold the larger structure and the price will not re-enter. In this context, the market would continue to show strength since, beyond what happens after the breakout, the price's inability to re-enter the range again is the definitive sign that the trend movement will most likely continue. Here we would face the problem of how to enter the market in that particular action. We have a potential larger cumulative scheme that is skewing the main context, and at the same time we have a smaller distributional scheme that tells us about bearish control in the shorter term. The problem is that the minor distributive scheme is something confirmed since it has had the effect of the downward movement; but the larger cumulative scheme is still potential based on the level of development that has taken place on the chart.

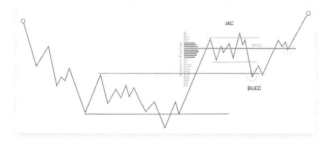

As always, we have various options to face a situation like this, from entering the market like any other structure without taking into account all this information; until the trading is discarded and remain outside the market. The intermediate strategy that I like to implement is to wait for the breakout and test of the control zone of that minor distributive structure of the JAC that has caused the bearish movement. And this control zone can be specifically identified by means of the VPOC of the volume profile of the structure.

We know that this structure has generated interest. There is participation by the agents and in a certain way it represents the bearish control of the market in the shortest term. We want to enter in favor of the potential accumulation that we have below, but without facing in advance that bearish control of the minor distribution that we have above. The solution would be to wait for said control to breakout, and an initial trace of this breakout is that the price manages to position itself above the VPOC of the structure. From that moment we can give greater confidence to the trading and start looking for our entry trigger.

Which Trading Level To Prioritize: Wyckoff Structure or Volume Profile

This is one of the big confusions faced by the trader who combines structure analysis together with volume profiling.

On the one hand, we know the importance of the trading levels that identify the extremes of the structure. These price inflection points generate the creation of the most relevant trading areas in the market based on the principle of auction and counterpart between the agents: the liquidity zones. As we already know, imbalances between supply and demand are expected to be generated in these areas that can provide us with trading opportunities.

On the other hand, as we have just studied throughout the entire book, we know the importance of volume in today's markets, how more and more large traders use trading levels to place their orders, generating thus, new areas of liquidity where, of course, imbalances are also expected to occur.

With this basic reasoning, it is logical that doubts arise about which levels are more important, if those of the structure itself, or those of the volume profile. The answer, how could it be otherwise, is both. Both levels create zones of liquidity; both levels create a zone of potential imbalance between buyers and sellers; In short, both levels create areas that can provide us with trading opportunities.

Therefore, it is best to have identified all these trading levels to make our decisions on them. It will ultimately be the price that will confirm to us which level is more important in that particular market condition. We must not get ahead of ourselves, our way of reading the market is reactive and here lies the importance of the appearance of our entry trigger as the last trace of the intention of the large traders in that direction.

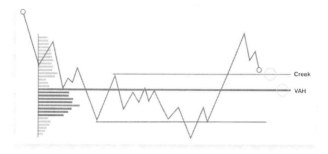

To land it with an example, if we are in a potential bullish breakout, our task as analysts is to identify the trading levels below which the price is likely to visit in order to carry out the confirmation test. In this case, they will be, first of all, the Creek of the structure, an old resistance that has now become a potential support; and the volume profile's Value Area High (VAH), the trading level that corresponds to the high end of the value area.

Once this is done, we only have to analyze the action of the market at those levels that we have identified and look for the entry trigger on them. Price could come to our first trading level and not develop the trigger, and instead go visit the second trading level lower where it may or may not now do so.

There is no one level better or more important than the other. On occasions and due to market conditions, the imbalance will take place on the level of the structure, while on other occasions it will be the most determining volume profile. It is not about guessing anything, just following the price.

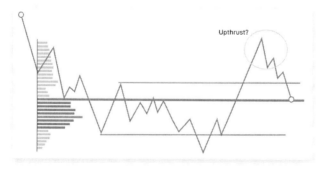

The problem that can be raised now is what feeling the market leaves us in case the price goes to look for the Value Area High instead of the Creek. At that point the market will have broken through the level of the structure and visually it might look like we are in for an Upthrust rather than an actual breakout. How to proceed then?

In the first place, it analyzes as objectively as possible the previous behavior of the market and the traces that it has been leaving us. It evaluates if it is offering us the best possible context (genuine structure plus trading trinomial) and if so, it simply waits to see the reaction of the price on the VAH. If your entry trigger appears you should take the trade.

But as almost always, there is another alternative. If the trading does not give you confidence for having crossed the Creek, wait for a second entry after recovering it again. In other words, it only assesses the possibility of entering the market after having seen that first reaction on the VAH that pushes the price back out of the range. From there you may want to wait for a new trigger to appear or enter the market directly.

Another possibility is to reapply active pyramiding-type management. If our entry trigger appears on the VAH we will enter with a percentage of the total position there; and in case the price breaks the Creek again, we will consider completing the total size of the position.

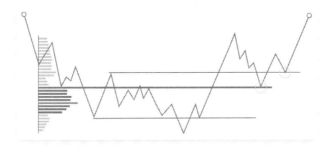

Free gift #5: Videos:

Auction Theory + Wyckoff Methodology

Which trading levels to prioritize

To complement the content in this section, I'm providing you with two videos where I explain the relationship between Auction Theory and the Wyckoff methodology. I cover the trading levels you should prioritize when considering not only the levels identified based on Wyckoff structures but also the trading zones according to the Volume Profile tool.

You can access from this link: https://tradingwyckoff.com/book-2/

or by scanning this QR code directly::

PART 6. CASE STUDIES

In this last part we are going to see in detail some real examples where the theoretical concepts presented previously are put into practice.

As I always say, what is really interesting about this type of example is to observe how the market tends to present the same structures but in a different way depending on the moment. This is what we mean when we declare that we must give the market "flexibility" in the development of structures.

This is something that, at this point, you should have internalized by now. The Wyckoff methodology is not about labeling all movements almost like a robot. It doesn't make any sense and we've already explained why. It is about analyzing the actions of the market in the most objective way possible (both what it does and what it fails to do) in order to grant greater control to buyers or sellers.

In addition, this section will be useful to see how the reading of the Volume Profile and the Order Flow is incorporated into the trading plan.

Euro/Dollar ($6E)

Chart on July 2, 3 and 6, 2020. Range context, operative in the extreme; more trend context, trading away from the value area.

This example is very representative of almost everything studied since it is full of interesting details.

In the first place we see the stop of the bearish movement (SC, AR, ST) beginning from there a new context of lateralization or balance. The AU already suggests to us in Phase B a buying intention by managing to do a test at the maximum of the structure. Highs of the structure whose nature is a LVN (Low Volume Node) as reflected in the profile of the first day. LVN that repeatedly acts as a rejection zone causing the price to turn until it finally breaks through it quickly. The Spring plus its test start the upward imbalance moving the market higher with relative ease.

Putting the magnifying glass on that potential Spring action on the trace chart, we see how the turn pattern in favor of the buyers is produced, represented by the rotation in the Delta (-240 to +183). In this first action, it should be noted that in the bearish candlestick there is no clear process of possible absorption, as we suggest you look for; but this is the reality of the market. We will not always see the theoretical patterns represented in the same way and the case is perfect to exemplify the need to grant flexibility to the market and be prepared for anything.

Beyond not having seen this process of potential absorption, the objective is that after a candlestick with a wide bearish range and high volume, the price has no continuity and turns with the same aggressiveness to the upside (effort/result divergence).

Very clearly the following action presented as a continuation pattern with the creation of the control plus the test. The control would be reflected by the maximum trading area within the bullish candlestick. We see how the price is going to develop the test just in that area and from there continue the upward imbalance.

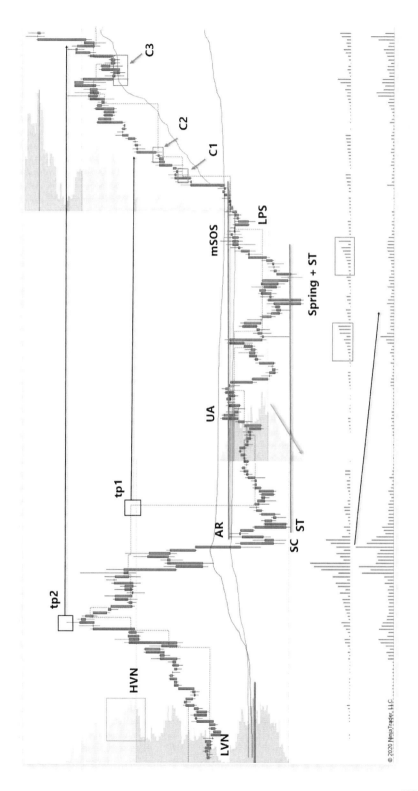

179

In addition to the price dynamics mentioned within the range, other signals are also observed in the volume, such as the decrease throughout its development, the appearance of a greater presence of Weis buyer; as well as the finished auction reading that we can make of the profile of day 3. That the volume represents a potential auction finished in confluence with a potential Spring is a very interesting signal to assume it as a lack of interest to continue falling.

Another very striking point of interest is the continuations that occur once the price is far from the value area and in a bullish trend context. Here the VPOC migration concept appears to support possible entries. We see how after the migrations the price continues its upward development (C1 and C2) almost immediately. It is a very useful input for this type of context. In the third continuation (C3) the market will visit one of the most important trading levels, the weekly VWAP, to develop a new bullish momentum from there.

With respect to the objectives, the first (tp1) to take into account would be that old zone of high negotiation (High Volume Node) that also left a DevelopingVPOC. And without more volume references to the left, subsequent objectives would go through identifying liquidity zones as relevant previous highs (tp2).

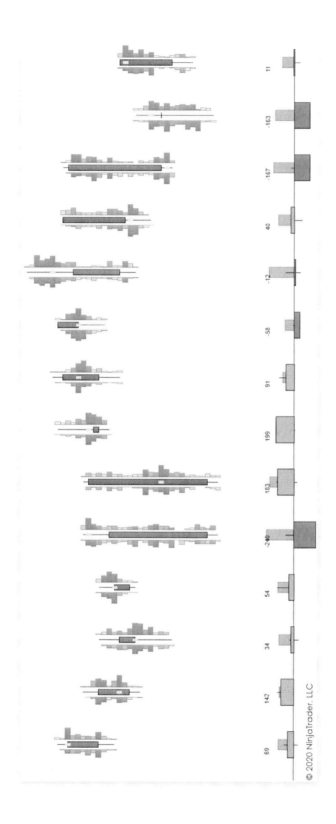

Pound/Dollar ($6B)

Trading profile chart week June 29 to July 3, 2020. Range context, trading inside; more context of trend, operative interacting with the value area.

In this case, the trading profile configured for the volume traded during the previous week has been used. As has already been mentioned, there is no better profile than another and it is therefore the trader's choice of the trading style that he wants to develop. The important thing is that the profile you decide to work on is complete to avoid confusion when current levels are modified.

In the first red box we would be in an trading position waiting for our input trigger. We are inside the value area but interacting just above the VPOC of the profile, so our bias at that point, being above said VPOC, should be in favor of the bullish continuation.

The price develops a minor structure and in a position of potential Spring coincides with a test at the trading level. From there, a first upward imbalance is generated that causes the profile to breakout at its upper part. Very visual how the bullish Weis stands out signaling that high participation in the breakout move; and how the following action denotes a lack of interest in the movement.

Just at that precise moment, at the end of the breakout movement, the trader who handles the tools proposed in this methodology should necessarily be favoring the bullish continuation. Basically because we have just seen a minor accumulation structure that has managed to breakout upwards, thus suggesting that the control is apparently on the side of the buyers.

As suggested in the trading checklist, we already have the first point resolved, which is: what do we want to do, whether to buy or sell. In this case and as we have just argued, we want to favor buying. Now we would need to answer point number two on the checklist, which is: where are we going to want to buy. We have to identify the level where we are going to be waiting for the price. In this example we have a very important confluence zone: the Value Area High of the broken weekly profile, the weekly VWAP (green line) and the upper end of the previous accumulation structure (Creek).

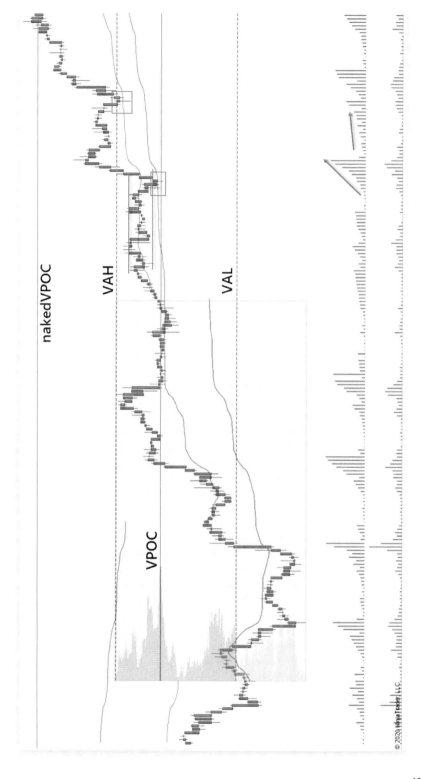

The identification of the second point of the checklist leads us immediately to the third, which is the setting of the scenario. In this case, since we are already in favor of the trading level, we would be waiting for a single movement for the price to position itself in our trading zone.

Once the price has arrived there, we would have to finally wait for the development of our entry trigger, which is part of step number four of the checklist. In this example we have used the Footprint to visualize the flow of orders and it has allowed us to see the entry of aggressive buyers represented on those two candlesticks with a positive delta of 685 and 793 that have also left imbalances in the ASK column. We would already have our checklist completed and therefore ready to send the orders to enter the market.

The recommended position management would be to place a buy stop order at the breakout of the bullish candlestick, with the stop loss on the low of the bearish candlestick. Returning to the previous chart, we would need to identify some interesting trading level on which to take profits or, failing that, some previous maximum that establishes a clear liquidity zone for us. In this case, further to the left we would have identified an old VPOC not yet tested (nakedVPOC).

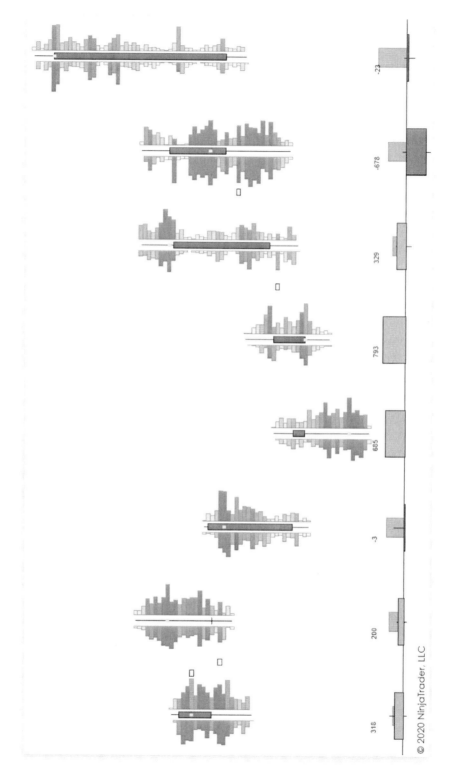

185

S&P500 Index ($ES)

Chart day July 17, 2020. Range context, trading within the range. Bullish reversal principle.

In the first 15-minute time frame we see the price exit below the value area of the previous day to begin to develop a new range in that area.

Initially and favoring the trading principle of bearish continuity, unless a longer-term context had biased us differently, we should have been willing to favor entering shorts in a potential test of the Value Area Low of the previous session's profile. .

Instead, what is observed is that the price manages to re-enter that value area and does so preceded by a false breakout to the lows that causes the upward movement. Here is reflected the importance of managing different scenarios depending on how the price behaves and of making a continuous evaluation of the movements.

If we look closely at the chart, after re-entering the Value Area, the price goes back to test the area where the VWAPs converge. Perhaps that test, due to the fact that it was slightly below the VAL, would not have given us all the confidence to trade it for buy; but the opportunity appears next when the price recovers the VA again and now it does leave a test inside.

In the following chart of less time (5 minutes) we see this action in greater detail. Here the structure under the Wyckoff methodology is already more recognizable. Although the stop of the downward movement is not very genuine, we see some lateralization and the Spring more test that originate the upward breakout. Again, the visualization of the Weis waves indicator is very useful, suggesting the institutional support of the movement. After the breakout, I do not re-enter the range accepting these levels.

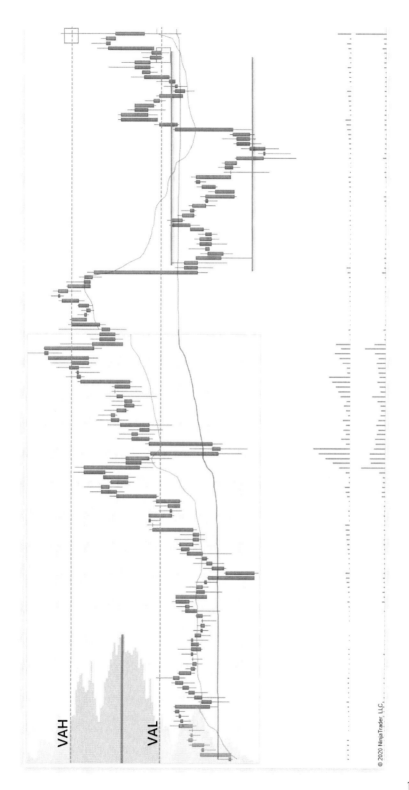

At the moment when we find ourselves in a situation of potential BUEC to provoke the upward imbalance, we are already waiting for the appearance of our entry trigger that allows us to launch the orders to buy.

It is therefore time to, if anything, begin to visualize the Footprint chart in search of that reversal pattern that alerts us to the imbalance in favor of speculators who are opening buy positions.

We see exactly that represented in the box indicated. Beyond the fact that the potential absorption is visual, the imbalance that is reflected in that bullish candlestick is more relevant, with a volume that is relatively higher than the average and with a comparatively very positive delta. After seeing this, it would certainly be time to send the buy order.

As an objective, we would firstly have the opposite end of the value area, in this case the Value Area High, a level that also converges, as can be seen in the second chart, with an old VPOC zone.

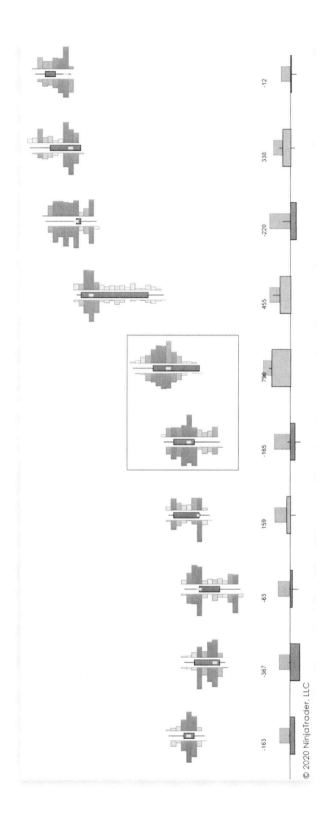

189

CANADIAN DOLLAR ($6C)

Chart of the day July 22, 2020. Range context, trading at the extremes.

The price begins the session the following day within the value area of the previous day, where it begins to lateralize, suggesting a total balance between buyers and sellers. The valuations of the agents that are trading at that moment are very similar, which causes a continuous rotation around the central zone.

With this base context; and under the hypothesis that the market continues in this state of balance, that no new information arrives that makes the participants change their valuations, the trading principle to work is to look for the reversal in the extremes; that is, look for buying when the price interacts with the low part of the value (Value Area Low) and selling on the high part (Value Area High).

Therefore, we are now in a position to propose the scenarios. We know what we want to do (buy or sell) and we know the exact location where we will wait for the price to look for the entry trigger. This means having a plan and not following the price reactively and by momentum.

As seen on the chart, the price is finally going to visit the bottom of the value area. It performs a very precise test and from there it launches towards the opposite end. We could label this movement within the events of the Wyckoff methodology as a potential Spring since it would be found false breakout the lows of that small structure that has been generated during the two days.

At that precise moment, it may be useful to visualize the order flow chart to confirm or not our buy entry trigger. We are in the right location and; As we know that the price could delay a little more before turning around, or even continue with the bearish development, we need to see the aggressive buy entry above that area to determine the possible start of the imbalance to the upside.

And just in the location of the potential Spring we see the appearance of this imbalance on the ASK column, which could suggest the entry of

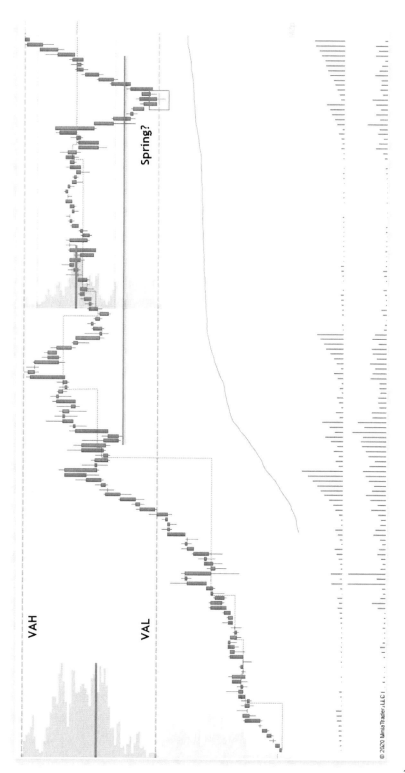

speculators in buying. It would be the signal we look for before proceeding to send the orders.

As we can see, the price subsequently launches to the opposite extreme, crossing the entire value area. It is an example of operations under the 80% Market Profile principle. Principle that suggests that; In the event that the price attempts to breakout out of a value area and fails, re-entering again, the price has an 80% chance of reaching the opposite end of said value area. Although this strategy was originated for Market Profile, the same principle can be used working with Volume Profile due to the similarities of their theories.

Therefore, taking profit in this case would be very clear: when performing a test on the Value Area High of the trading profile. In case the price reaches such a point, the situation would be very interesting because we would come from potential Spring; which, as we all know, is the event that unbalances the control of the upward structure. Therefore, if they are correct in the analysis, it would still have to develop at least one more upward movement.

That would be the route map that we would be driving, but without a doubt that VAH test is our first management area. Here you could decide to close the entire position or leave a contract, but what we should do at least yes or yes is to protect the position; that is, move the stop loss to the entry level (what is known as Breakeven).

POUND/DOLLAR ($6B)

Day chart 03 August 2020. Trend context, trading interacting with the value area.

Example of intraday trading favoring the context of the shortest term, in this case, using the trading profile of the previous session.

The fact that we use profiles of previous sessions as a framework on which to base our operations does not mean that the principles of the Wyckoff methodology are left aside. Well, as we can see, in essence it is the same thing, the only difference is found in the temporality used.

Any Wyckoff trader with some experience could identify a structure and label all the events that the methodology teaches us within that profile. Moreover, the moment in which it is indicated as the area where to look for the entry trigger, the most astute analysts will have already been able to identify a new structure. This is the important thing, the context, what are you going to favor (buy or sell) based on what the price does.

In this example, after seeing that we come from a distributive structure, initially we will be favoring the incorporation in shorts. The next step would be to identify at what point we are going to wait for the price to proceed with the search for the trigger. Here, the first interesting area is in the Value Area Low of the profile.

During the current day the market begins to lateralize creating new value in that area. This is a sign of acceptance of the prior distribution, so we can add one more input in favor of our bearish scenario.

Once the price is found in the proposed trading zone, we have an important confluence of events since, on the one hand, we would be developing a test of the old broken value area; and also said movement could be part of a false breakout of that new structure that would be forming.

It would be the ideal time to analyze the Order Flow chart and see what is happening inside the candlesticks and if our entry trigger is confirmed in the shortest term.

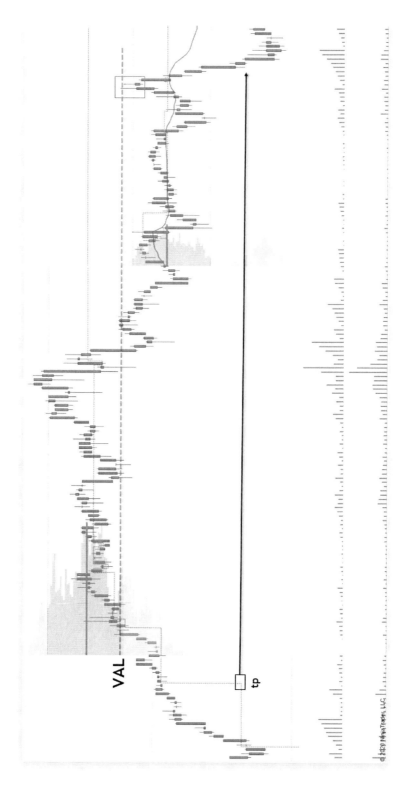

And right in that location what we see is this. A bearish turn with a lot of selling aggressiveness. Already in the last bullish candlestick we can suggest some absorption of buying evidenced by the high volume, the large number of executions that take place in the ASK column and the lack of bullish continuity reflected in the upper wick.

Following this, a large share of selling, evidenced mainly by the large negative delta, suggests a selling initiative and the possible beginning of the bearish imbalance. The following bearish candlestick would serve as a definitive confirmation of the seller's control: a wide-range candlestick, with good volume and a low close, which we know by Wyckoff methodology as SOWbar (Sign of Weakness Bar).

These examples are very instructive to see the infinite ways in which the same action, as in this case it is the bearish turn, can appear on the chart. Sometimes both the absorption process and the initiative process will be very clear; and other times it won't. Given that we are in a particular trading zone and that we have the support of the context, it would be more interesting to prioritize the appearance of the initiative in favor of the direction that we expect the market to move over visualizing yes or yes the previous process of absorption, since as we see this does not always appear in the most genuine way.

Unlike the absorption process, the initiative would indeed be an essential action (for traders who decide to analyze the flow of orders), since ultimately we are waiting for those speculators to appear to definitively unbalance control.

Lastly, in this trading a possible Take Profit would be located at that old level that was VPOC and that by its very nature represents a high trading zone, even if it is in the shortest term.

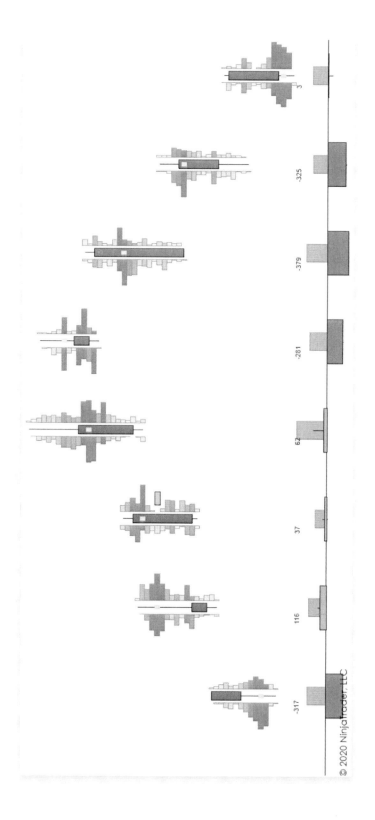

197

EURO/DOLLAR ($6E)

Day chart 31 August 2020. Range context, trading within the range. Failed reversal principle.

This type of trading usually presents greater confidence problems because initially we come from prioritizing the reversal scenario and then changing bias.

Also using the profile of the previous day as an trading basis, we see that on the last day the price tries to leave said value area at its upper part, causing a rejection and re-entering the range. At that point we start looking for the short incorporation favoring the reversal principle.

The failed reversal is a perfect example of why trading levels should be used to manage the position as price interacts with them. These are decisive areas and we do not know what will happen, therefore the only thing that is under our control is to minimize the risk of our trading.

If just above the identified trading zone we see a reversal like the one seen in the footprint chart, at least two decisions could be made in time. First of all, if we are short, we may want to close the position and prevent the Stop Loss from being touched even if it is already in a Breakeven position. This type of active management, at times like this, is very important as it will allow us to reduce risk even more, being able to scratch a few more points from the market. On the other hand, if the longer-term context accompanies you, you may want to enter the buy favoring this failed reversal principle.

In case of considering a buy, there is an interesting detail to take into account. As the entry trigger is below the weekly VWAP, it could be a good option to make such an trading with a lower leverage, for example, in a CFD market. It is a perfect example to assess the possibility of trading the same asset in different markets depending on the confidence that the trading in question grants us. If we find ourselves in a situation like this in which we observe such elements against the proposed scenario, the most advisable thing would be not to do it in a leveraged market such as the futures market; and on the contrary, go to a market that offers us a less leveraged type of trading such as CFDs.

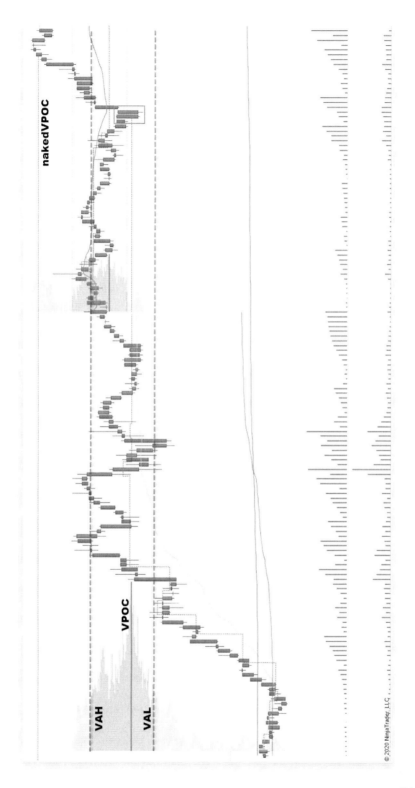

Going deeper into this concept of working with different brokers and markets, it is important to remember that you do not necessarily have to pigeonhole yourself into any particular type of trading. You may want to make shorter-term speculative trades by trading the asset in question on the futures market; and this is not incompatible with proposing scenarios that cover a longer period of time and carry out said medium-term operations using the CFDs already mentioned; and also to be able to carry out longer-term operations with cash shares or with exchange-traded investment funds (ETFs), for example.

This is one of the benefits of the methodology, its universality. His reading, being based on the true engine of the market, the continuous interaction between buyers and sellers, is equally valid regardless of the asset and time frame; with a single basic requirement that the particular asset has sufficient liquidity.

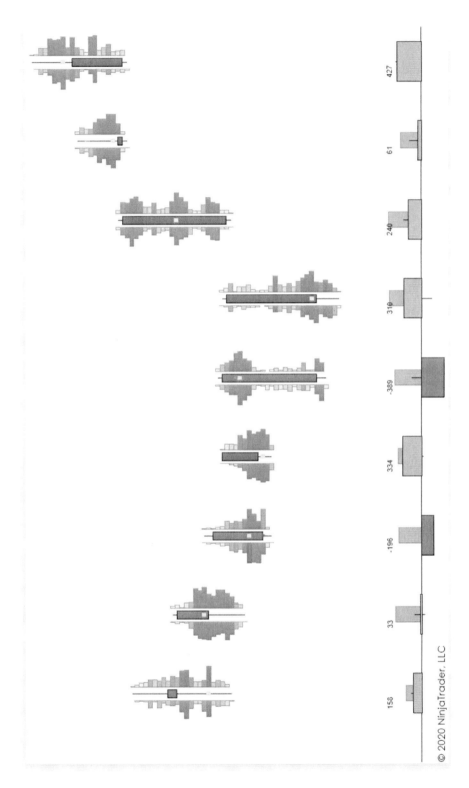

ACKNOWLEDGEMENTS

Congratulations. After reading this book you have now taken the first step. I sincerely hope that it has been of value to you and helped you build the foundations that will allow you to reach higher levels of performance as a trader or investor. The content is dense and nuanced. It is very difficult to acquire all the knowledge after a single reading, so I recommend that you review it again and take personal notes for a better understanding.

As you know, I continually carry out research and share additional information, so please write to me at **info@tradingwyckoff.com** so that I can include you in a new list and send you future updates of the content totally free of charge.

Also, if you would like a copy of the book in pdf so you can analyze the graphs in color send me an email and I will be happy to send it to you.

Twitter: twitter.com/RubenVillaENG

Youtube: youtube.com/RubenVillahermosa

Web: tradingwyckoff.com/en

Before you go, I wanted to ask you for one small favor. **Could you please consider posting a review on the platform? Posting a review is the best and easiest way to support the work of independent authors like me.** Your feedback will help me to keep writing the kind of books that will help you get the results you want. It would mean a lot to me to hear from you.

ABOUT THE AUTHOR

Rubén Villahermosa Chaves has been an independent analyst and trader in the financial markets since 2016.

He has extensive knowledge of technical analysis in general and has specialized in methodologies that analyze the interaction between supply and demand, reaching a high degree of training in this area. In addition, he is passionate about automated trading and has dedicated part of his training to how to develop trading strategies based on quantitative analysis.

He tries to bring value to the trading community by disseminating the knowledge acquired from principles of honesty, transparency and responsibility.

BOOKS BY THE AUTHOR

Trading and Investing for beginners

The financial markets are controlled by large financial institutions which allocate enormous resources and hire the best engineers, physicists and mathematicians to appropriate the money belonging to the other participants. And you're going to have to fight them.

Your only chance is to somehow level the playing field. Instead of fighting them you need to try to trade alongside them. To do this, you need to become the complete trader and develop and follow the 3 main principles that will largely determine whether you are successful or not:

WHAT WILL YOU LEARN?

- Basic and advanced concepts on **Financial Education**.

- Theoretical fundamentals on **Financial Markets**.

- 3 high level T**echnical Analysis** methodologies:

    - Price Action.

    - Volume Spread Analysis.

    - Wyckoff Methodology.

- Advanced **Risk Management** Techniques.

- Principles of **Emotional Management** applied to trading.

- How to make a professional **Business Management**.

- How to start from scratch, **from Theory to Practice**.

All this knowledge will allow you to:

- Improve the health of your **economy**.

- Understand **how the stock markets work**.

- Learn 4 **winning trading strategies**.

- Implement **solid money management methods**.

- Develop a **statistical and objective mindset**.

- Make step by step your own **trading plan**.

- Implement **trade record** and periodic evaluation.

- Discover resources for obtaining **investment ideas.**

- Manage the organization of assets through **watch lists**.

The Wyckoff Methodology in Depth

How to trade financial markets logically

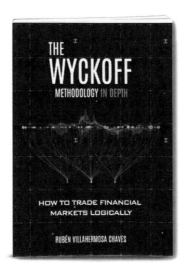

The Wyckoff method is a technical analysis approach to trading in financial markets based on the study of the relationship between the forces of supply and demand.

The premise is simple: When large operators want to buy or sell, they execute processes that leave their mark that can be seen on the charts through price and volume.

The Wyckoff method is based on identifying this intervention by professionals to try to elucidate who has control of the market in order to trade alongside them.

WHAT WILL YOU LEARN?

- **Theoretical principles** of how markets work:
  - How price moves.
  - The 3 fundamental laws.
  - The processes of accumulation and distribution.
- Exclusive t**rading elements** of the Wyckoff methodology:
  - Events.
  - Phases.
  - Structures.
- **Advanced concepts** for experienced Wyckoff traders.
- Resolution of **frequent doubts**.
- **Trading and position management**.

All this knowledge will allow you to:

- Identify **institutional money** participation.
- Determine market **context and sentiment**.
- Knowing the **high probability trading zones**.
- To propose scenarios on the basis of a defined **roadmap**.
- Manage **risk and trade** appropriately.

Wyckoff 2.0: Structures, Volume Profile and Order Flow

Combining the logic of the Wyckoff Methodology and the objectivity of the Volume Profile

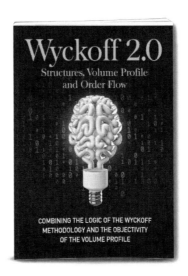

Wyckoff 2.0 is the natural evolution of the Wyckoff Methodology. It is about bringing together two of the most powerful concepts of Technical Analysis: the best price analysis together with the best volume analysis.

This book has been written for experienced and demanding traders who want to make a quality leap in their trading through the study of advanced tools for volume analysis such as Volume Profile and Order Flow.

The universality of this method allows its implementation to all types of traders, both short, medium and long term; although daytraders may obtain a greater benefit.

WHAT WILL YOU LEARN?

- Advanced knowledge of how financial markets work: **the current trading ecosystem.**

- Tools created by and for **professional traders**.

- Essential and complex concepts of **Volume Profile**.

- Fundamentals and objective analysis of **Order Flow**.

- Evolved concepts of **Position Managemen**t.

All this knowledge will allow you to:

- **Discovering the B side of the financial market**:

    - The different participants and their interests.

    - The nature of decentralized markets (OTC).

    - What are Dark Pools and how they affect the market.

- How the **matching of orders** takes place and the problems of their analysis.

- Knowing the Trading principles with **Value Areas**.

- How to implement **Order Flow** patterns in intraday Trading.

- Build step by step your own **trading strategy**:

    - Context analysis.

    - Identification of Trading areas.

    - Scenario planning.

    - Position management.

AUTHOR'S COURSES

Advanced Wyckoff Course + Volume Profile

Learn in a simple way advanced concepts of the Wyckoff Method.

I will teach you unique concepts that will make you an expert in the Wyckoff Method and take your analysis and trading to the next level.

It is the right complement for those Wyckoff traders who have already laid the theoretical foundations and want to make a quality leap in their analysis and trading.

▶ Who is this course for?

This course has been created for traders who are familiar with the fundamentals of the Wyckoff Method. It is not a course for beginners.

▶ Why this course?

Quite simply because the subject is being taught incorrectly. The Wyckoff Method is not about establishing a robotic pattern and nothing more. The

Wyckoff Method is way of understanding what is really happening in the market.

▶ **What will you learn?**

Based on the rules of logic and objectivity, you will learn to really understand the principles of the Wyckoff Method, as well as the real underlying advantage that it can offer.

All this from a practical point of view, using a multitude of examples that will help your understanding.

In addition, you will receive access to the **Volume Profile Course**, new content that will make you an expert in the use of the Volume Profile.

The combination of the **Wyckoff Method + Volume Profile** is the definitive step for the most demanding traders, and very few know the advantage that the correct combination of these two tools can bring.

What should you know about this course?

▶ **Money back guarantee.** I am so confident that I will bring you tremendous value that I offer a full money back guarantee.

▶ **Discord.** You will have access to a premium Discord room to connect with other members of the community.

▶ **Updates**. The course will be constantly updated and new valuable content will be added,

▶ **Permanent support.** You will have direct contact with Rubén via email or Discord to solve all your doubts.

Go to the course page for more information:

https://cursowyckoff.rubenvillahermosa.com/course/advanced-wyckoff-course

BIBLIOGRAPHY

Aldridge, I. (2010). High-Frequency Trading: A Practical Guide to Algorithmic Strategies and Trading Systems. John Wiley & Sons Ltd.

Alexander Trading, LLC. (2008). Practical Trading Applications of Market Profile.

Brooks, A. (2012). Trading Price Action Trends. Wiley Trading.

Daniels Trading. (2018). Types of Futures Trades: Basis, Spread, Hedging. Obtained from https://www.danielstrading.com/2018/02/06/types-futures-trades-basis-spread-hedgingç

Delgado-Bonal, A. (2019). Quantifying the randomness of the stock markets. Obtained from Scientific Reports: https://doi.org/10.1038/s41598-019-49320-9

Diaman Partners Ltd. (2017). Are financial markets Random or Deterministic? Obtained from http://blog.diamanpartners.com/are-financial-markets-random-or-deterministic

Edwin Oswaldo Gil Mateus, H. D. (2016). Mercados financieros, eficiencia y adaptación.

Obtained from http://dx.doi.org/10.19052/ed.3735

Hawkins, P. S. (2003). Steidlmayer on Markets: Trading with Market Profile. John Wiley & Sons.

Healthy Markets Association. (2015). The dark side of the pools: What investors should learn from regulators´actions.

James F. Dalton, E. T. (1993). Mind over markets.

Jones, D. L. (1993). Value-Based Power Trading – Using the overlay demand curve to pintpoint trends & predict market turns. Probus Publishing Company.

Jones, D. L. (2002). Auction Market Theory. Cisco Futures.

Keppler, J. (2011). Profit With the Market Profile: Identifying Market Value in Real Time.

Marketplace Books Inc.

Koy, P. S. (1986). Market & Markets Logics. The Porcupine Press. Lewis, M. (2018). Flash Boys. Norton & Company.

Lloret, V. M. (2016). La guía the Tradingway.

Lo, A. W. (2017). Adaptive Markets: Financial Evolution at the Speed of Thought. Princeton University Press.

Nasdaq. (2019). Total markets. A blueprint for a better tomorrow.

Patterson, S. (2013). DARK POOLS: The Rise of the Machine Traders and the Rigging of the U.S. Stock Market. Random House LCC US.

Peter Gomber, B. A. (2011). High-Frequency Trading.

Piras, A. F. (2018). Non-random behavior in financial markets. Obtained from https://www.researchgate.net/publication/322820666_Non_Random_Patterns_in_Financial_Markets

SEC. (2011). Pub. No. 141 (3/11) Trading Basics. understanding the Different Ways to Buy and sell stock.

SIFMA Insights. (2019). Electronic Trading Market Structure Primer.

Tapiero, P. d. (2014). Is there light in dark trading? A GARCH analysis of transactions in dark pools.

Valtos, M. (2015). Trading Order Flow - Understanding & Profiting From Market Generated Information As It Occurs.

Verniman. (2020). Futures Trading. Obtenido de https://verniman.blogspot.com/

Warner, J. (2019). High-frequency trading explained: why has it decreased? Obtained from https://www.ig.com/en-ch/trading-strategies/high-frequency-trading-explained--why-has-it-decreased--181010

Wedow, M. P. (2017). Dark pools in European equity.

Wikipedia. (2021). Algorithmic trading. Obtained from https://en.wikipedia.org/wiki/Algorithmic_trading

Made in United States
North Haven, CT
30 November 2024

61221207R00122